CHEESE & WINE

Cheese & Wine

A Guide to Selecting, Pairing, and Enjoying

JANET FLETCHER

photographs by Victoria Pearson

SAN FRANCISCO

This Chronicle Books LLC edition published in 2007.

Library of Congress Cataloging-in-Publication Data available.

ISBN-13: 978-0-8118-5743-7

Manufactured in China

10 9 8 7 6 5 4 3

Chronicle Books LLC
680 Second Street
San Francisco, California 94107
www.chroniclebooks.com

Design: *Gretchen Scoble, Pamela Geismar*
Typesetting: *Blue Friday*
Stylist: *Ann Johnstad*
Photographer's Assistant: *Jon Nakano*
Stylist's Assistant: *Susan Robohm*

The publisher wishes to acknowledge Williams-Sonoma for providing many of the beautiful cheese knives, serving boards and platters, plates, glasses, and linens pictured throughout this book. Additionally, thanks to Pottery Barn for providing plates and a serving platter.

⟵ PAGE 2, LEFT TO RIGHT: Bayley Hazen Blue, Brillat-Savarin

Contents

Cheeses by Type

TOP TO BOTTOM: *Cantal, Pleasant Ridge Reserve* >

Cheese and Wine: A Time-Tested Marriage

Over the centuries, humans have learned to preserve nature's seasonal bounty for the times when nature is not so generous. The abundant milk that a cow gives in summer becomes cheese for the winter months. Fresh grapes, which last only days, become wine for future enjoyment. In the temperate climates that nurture both grapevines and dairy animals, it is not surprising that cheese and wine are savored together. Both have long been the daily sustenance of farmers in Spain, France, Greece, and Italy who think of wine and cheese not as fancy foods for entertaining, but as the wholesome heart of an everyday meal.

In America, cheese and wine are too often seen as party food, as something served at a gallery opening or bought only when company is coming. That's a shame, because although cheese and wine certainly belong on the table when you are entertaining, they are also a pair worth making part of every day.

European cultures provide many models. Who hasn't sighed with pleasure at the sight of the cheese cart in a fine French restaurant? In French homes, the cheese course is more modest—perhaps a couple of local cheeses from the farmers' market and a baguette—but the daily ritual provides an opportunity to enjoy the last of the dinner wine and linger a little longer at the table. In Spain, friends meet at tapas bars after work for a glass of sherry and a few slices of Manchego. Italians may end a meal with a few chunks of Parmigiano-Reggiano drizzled with balsamic vinegar, or a wedge of Gorgonzola and a glass of *passito*, a luscious dessert wine.

These time-tested matches never disappoint, but there are many more to explore. With this book, you can begin that voyage of discovery, treating yourself and your guests to those pleasurable moments when a good cheese meets the right wine.

< *Humboldt Fog*

STRATEGIES FOR HARMONY

Whether you are choosing wine to accompany a platter of cheeses, or selecting cheeses to enjoy with a favorite wine, the objective is the same: to "do no harm" to the taste of the wine. When we talk about a successful wine and cheese match, we mean that the cheese or cheeses do not diminish our pleasure in the wine. The wine tastes just as good with the cheese as it does on its own. Occasionally, but not often, a cheese may even enhance a wine.

On the other hand, we rarely need to think about how a wine may affect a cheese. The cheese is the dominant partner in this pairing, and your perception of it is probably not going to change, no matter what wine you are drinking. For the best outcome, consider the following elements when making your selections:

Texture. Is the cheese creamy and palate-coating or firm and dry? Is the wine a crisp and refreshing Sauvignon Blanc? Or is it a full-bodied and velvety Viognier? Matching textures can be a good strategy, such as pairing a buttery Camellia with a creamy Chardonnay. But contrast also works, as when a *triple-crème* Brillat-Savarin meets a palate-cleansing sparkling wine.

Intensity. For delicate wines, choose delicate cheeses. More robust wines can handle cheeses with more concentrated flavors. That's why youthful cheeses—fresh goat cheeses, for example—tend to go with youthful wines, like a young Sauvignon Blanc or Chenin Blanc. Likewise, aged cheeses, such as Parmigiano-Reggiano, with their heightened intensity, do best with relatively big, full-bodied wines. One exception: a bold blue cheese may seem to call for a powerhouse red, but that combination is often disastrous. Instead, look to a sweet dessert wine to counter the strength of blue cheeses and avert a flavor clash with the blue mold.

LEFT TO RIGHT: *L'Édel de Cléron and Reblochon* >

Acidity. Cheeses and wines both have acidity. When you have a cheese of pronounced acidity, such as a Cheddar or Valençay, it is a good idea to counter it with a wine of firm acidity, too.

Sweetness. Cheeses are not literally sweet. With the exception of very fresh cheeses, such as cottage cheese, which may still have unfermented lactose (milk sugar), cheese has no measurable sugar. Nevertheless, we perceive some cheeses as having a sweet or caramel-like finish. Boerenkaas and Lincolnshire Poacher leave this impression. A nutty, off-dry sherry or Madeira can be particularly pleasing with such cheeses.

Mold. The veins of mold in blue cheeses strip most dry white and red wines of their fruit. A sweet wine is almost always the better choice. The more pungent and salty the blue, the richer the dessert wine should be. Curiously, sparkling wines can hold their own with many blue cheeses.

Region. Serving cheese and wine from the same region satisfies us on an emotional level. Indeed, Vella's Dry Monterey Jack with Sonoma County Zinfandel, or Sainte-Maure de Touraine with Vouvray reminds us that some of the best matches are local ones. But don't rely on this guideline uncritically. Many cheeses come from areas where wine isn't produced, and regional matches are not always the best ones.

A few wines present greater challenges for the cheese enthusiast. Heavily oaked wines, especially oaky whites, rarely show well with cheese. Tannic reds also call for caution. They work best with dry, aged cheeses, such as Parmigiano-Reggiano or an aged Manchego or Pecorino Toscano, but are rarely totally satisfying partners for cheese.

< Valdeón

PLANNING THE CHEESE COURSE

A cheese course doesn't have to be elaborate to be inviting. A single carefully chosen cheese, in perfect condition, is more alluring than a tray loaded with underripe or uninspired selections. A glistening wedge of Manchego served with green olives makes an eye-catching cheese course before dinner. At the end of a meal, a slice of Great Hill Blue garnished with honey and toasted hazelnuts can stand in for dessert.

For most occasions, three cheeses make an ample and generous cheese course for a dinner party. It can be awkward and slow, at a seated dinner, to pass a board with many more selections than that. For a buffet or stand-up party, where the cheese board isn't passed, you can fill it with as many cheeses as your budget allows.

If you are serving more than one cheese, plan your purchases so that you have a complementary assortment. One approach is to assemble cheeses that offer diversity: fresh cheeses and aged ones; mild cheeses and strong ones; a mix of cow's, sheep's, and goat's milk cheeses; or a variety of styles, such as a bloomy rind, a washed rind, a blue, and a Cheddar. Also consider diversity of shape and color: a tray with a round, a wedge, and a pyramid is more inviting than a tray with three wedges.

Diversity ensures that there is something for everyone and a variety of taste experiences on the tray. On the other hand, it can be enlightening to offer two or three similar cheeses for comparison, such as two aged sheep's milk cheeses, one from Vermont and one from Spain. Wine enthusiasts often compare Pinot Noir or Cabernet Sauvignon from different regions. Why not apply the same principle to cheese?

If the cheese course is part of a multicourse meal, plan on about two ounces of cheese per person. However, you may want to purchase more to have a bountiful-looking tray. If you are hosting a dinner party for eight people, for example, the group will probably consume about a pound of cheese. But a tray

LEFT TO RIGHT: *Munster-Géromé, Abondance, Monte Enebro* >

with three cheeses, each weighing a meager one-third pound, will look sad and stingy. Purchase enough so that each cheese has some stature.

Anyone who has traveled in France knows the appeal of the end-of-meal cheese course. In the choreography of a French meal, cheese typically follows the main course. A salad may accompany the cheese, or precede it. French hosts often save the finest wine of the evening for the cheese course, and many French dinners end here, with no dessert.

Americans, in contrast, are more inclined to enjoy their cheese before dinner, with a cocktail or the evening's first glass of wine. Either approach is correct. If you do serve cheese before the meal, it is wise to stay away from rich and creamy cheeses, such as Brillat-Savarin or Hudson Valley Camembert, and from cheeses with caramel notes, such as Boerenkaas. These cheeses can dull the appetite and are more appropriate for dessert. Dry, aged cheeses, such as Manchego, Montasio, or Dry Monterey Jack, have a salty concentration that, like salted nuts, makes them appealing before dinner.

What to serve with cheese? Truly, good cheese stands on its own and needs no accompaniment, not even bread. You will experience its character most fully when you enjoy it unadorned, with only a knife and fork. That said, many people do prefer eating cheese, especially a soft and creamy cheese or a pungent blue, with a slice of bread.

The best choice is a loaf that doesn't interfere with the flavor of the cheese. You can't go wrong with a plain, nonsourdough baguette or a French or Italian country loaf made of only flour, water, yeast, and salt. Breads with sugar, fat, herbs, or other embellishments are best avoided, although rare exceptions come to mind, such as walnut bread with goat's milk or blue cheeses.

Seasonal fresh fruits can accompany cheese or follow it. Figs with Gorgonzola or pears with an aged Pecorino Toscano successfully juxtapose sweet with salty. But because most fruits are high in acid and sugar, they can compromise the enjoyment of any dry wine selected to accompany the cheese.

< LEFT TO RIGHT: *Green Peppercorn Cone, Cashel Blue*

If you want to showcase the wine, save the fruit for afterward. Some other possible companions for cheese:

Dried fruits. In winter, dried figs, dates, pears, and plums are appealing with cheeses. Compotes, purees, and concentrated dried-fruit butters complement salty aged cheeses, such as mature Ossau-Iraty or Pecorino Toscano.

Honey. Strong blue cheeses are tamed by a drizzle of fragrant honey.

Chutney. A traditional partner for Cheddar, chutney also pairs well with aged sheep's milk cheeses.

Olives. Green or black olives provide a salty complement to fresh goat cheeses or Manchego before dinner.

Toasted nuts. Toasted almonds, walnuts, or hazelnuts are appropriate with virtually any cheese. Always toast nuts before serving to intensify their flavor.

LEFT TO RIGHT: Mimolette, Gorgonzola >

HANDLING AND SERVING CHEESE

Cheese always tastes best at room temperature. Flavors and aromas emerge that are muted when the cheese is cold, and the texture becomes more supple, especially in moist cheeses. A small refrigerated wedge needs about an hour to come to room temperature. Larger pieces require more time.

Unwrap the cheese when you remove it from the refrigerator to avoid trapping any moisture released as it warms. Protect the bare cheese from drying by covering it with a cheese dome, cake cover, or overturned bowl. Some blues "weep," or release moisture, as they warm; pat them dry with a paper towel before serving.

Well-made cheese is beautiful in its own right and needs little enhancement. However, a stylish platter or cheese board can make your cheese course more enticing. Choose a surface that is easy to cut on, such as wood, marble, granite, or a wicker tray with a glass insert. Don't crowd the cheeses, as guests need room to maneuver. If you have access to fresh grape or fig leaves, they make an attractive foundation for cheese.

Remove any paper or foil wrappers, but leave rinds in place. The rind is a natural wrap and is part of the visual appeal and integrity of the cheese. Guests can cut it away themselves if it is inedible or they choose not to eat it.

Offer a separate knife for each cheese to avoid cross contamination. Some aged cheeses with concentrated flavors, such as Comté, are delicious when shaved, so you may want to offer a cheese plane, too. Accompany Parmigiano-Reggiano with a blunt knife that breaks the cheese into chunks, as slicing it would compromise its texture. Many cookware stores sell the specially designed trowel-bladed implement used for serving Parmigiano-Reggiano in Italy.

When you are serving yourself from a cheese board, pause for a moment to consider the best way to make each cut. You want to leave the cheese looking attractive for the next guest, preferably as close as possible to its original shape. Ideally each person is able to share in every part of the cheese, from the rind

< TOP TO BOTTOM: *Humboldt Fog, Tumalo Tomme, Camembert*

to the core. Try to keep a wedge of Brie, for example, looking like a wedge by slicing lengthwise, not cutting across the pointed tip.

A cheese is never better than when it is first cut. Once a whole cheese is breached, it begins its inexorable decline. Quality suffers each time it goes in and out of the refrigerator, too, so it is best to buy only as much as you think you will eat fairly quickly and to store it properly.

If a cheese is wrapped in plastic film when you buy it, unwrap it when you get it home. Plastic film smothers cheese, making it hard for it to breathe and give off moisture. It can also impart an unpleasant flavor to the surface. You need to create a better home for your cheese, one that allows it to breathe, while still protecting it from the drying environment of the refrigerator.

High-moisture cheeses, such as Feta or fresh goat cheese, do well in an airtight plastic container. Otherwise, wrap all but the driest cheeses in waxed paper and place them in a lidded container. You can keep multiple cheeses in the same container, although blue cheeses should be kept separate to prevent their molds from traveling. You may also want to keep washed-rind cheeses separate to avoid imbuing other cheeses with their strong fragrance. Dry cheeses, such as Parmigiano-Reggiano, no longer have much moisture to lose, so a tight foil wrap is fine.

UNDER WIRE DOME: *L'Édel de Cléron*; UNDER GLASS, LEFT TO RIGHT: *Fiscalini Cheddar and Berkswell* >

Cheeses to Know

Some of the world's most beloved cheeses are profiled in the following pages, in alphabetical order. They come from many countries and represent many different styles, from mild goat cheeses to piquant blues. Some are ancient, others relatively new. Each profile offers a little history, a detailed sensory description, and a suggestion for complementary wines. With this information, you can always find a suitable cheese to accompany a favorite wine, or a wine to partner your chosen cheese.

ABONDANCE

(ah-bohn-DAHNCE)
Raw cow's milk
France

Made in the mountains of the Haute-Savoie, near the Swiss border, Abondance (pictured on pages 15, 92) benefits from a centuries-old ritual known as the transhumance, the seasonal movement of livestock to take advantage of mountain pastures. In late spring, once the snows have melted, the local cows are driven progressively up the mountains (on foot in the old days, by truck today) to feed on the fresh pasture along the way. By early autumn, when cold weather returns, they begin their descent, nourishing themselves on the now-regrown grasses. The milk from these pasture-fed cows produces the best cheese, experts say, surpassing the wheels made from the winter milk of cows fed on hay.

Today, most of the milk for Abondance is trucked to dairies for cheese production, but some wheels are still made on high-mountain farms. These *alpage* cheeses, as they are known, are the most prized and bear a blue label.

Wheels of Abondance weigh anywhere from fifteen to twenty-five pounds but are only about three inches high. You can recognize them by their convex sides, like a cinched waist. During the three- to seven-month aging, the wheels are repeatedly washed with brine that contains flavor-enhancing bacteria.

Abondance resembles a particularly mellow Gruyère. The crust is mottled with gold and gray molds; the interior is firm and smooth, ivory to pale yellow, with a few small eyes. Compared with Gruyère, which can be slightly grainy and biting, Abondance is supple, sweet, and fruity, with an aroma that hints of brown butter, light caramel, and grass.

WINES THAT WORK: *A nutty amontillado sherry will complement the brown-butter notes of the cheese; an Alsatian Pinot Gris has the flavor intensity to match its concentration.*

APPENZELLER

(APP-en-zell-er)
Raw or pasteurized cow's milk
Switzerland

Almost one thousand years ago, monks in northeastern Switzerland established the parish of Abbacella (abbot's cell), a name that evolved into Appenzell. The local farmers tithed their cheese to the church, so we know the monks ate well.

Today, Appenzeller is produced in seventy dairies, but only a handful still make the cheese with raw milk. The wheels weigh roughly twenty pounds and are about three inches tall, with a reddish brown natural rind. During their aging, a minimum of three months, they are repeatedly bathed with an herbal brine whose exact recipe is proprietary and differs from one cheesemaker to the next. Some are said to incorporate at least twenty herbs in their formula, or to use a local herbal liqueur or white wine. Notice the blue-gray line between the paste and the rind. The thicker it is, the more frequently the cheese was washed.

So-called Appenzeller Classic has been cellared for three months and bears a silver label. Surchoix wheels are at least four months old and bear a gold label. Cheeses matured for at least six months receive a black and gold label and the designation Extra. Highly regarded Swiss *affineur* (cheese ager) Rolf Beeler gives his raw-milk Appenzeller seven to nine months' aging, and his wheels are the crème de la crème. He puts his own paper label on them.

Appenzeller Extra is a compelling cheese, with aromas of roasted hazelnut and brown butter and some of the barnyard fragrance common to washed-rind cheeses. The interior is smooth and dense, butter colored to golden, with a few eyes. If you shave the cheese, it will melt on your tongue, delivering sweet and fruity flavors and a spicy finish.

WINES THAT WORK: *A fino or amontillado sherry will complement the cheese's nutty notes. Among white wines, look for a Pinot Gris with body and aromatic intensity. A medium-weight red, such as Merlot, can also be a good partner.*

APPLEBY'S CHESHIRE

Raw cow's milk
England

Documents confirm that the British were enjoying Cheshire as early as the eleventh century, probably making it England's oldest cheese. By the eighteenth century, it was more popular than Cheddar. Twelve hundred farms were still making Cheshire in the 1920s, but World War II and subsequent rationing devastated them, forcing many cheese-makers out of business and shifting production to factories. Today, Cheshire is largely an industrial cheese, a commodity that every British cheesemonger stocks but few praise.

Appleby's Cheshire is the shining exception. Lance and Lucy Appleby had been making traditional Cheshire on their farm since 1949, and watching their business dwindle as wholesalers shifted to the factory product. Their cheese cost more and required more careful handling than wholesalers were willing to provide. The couple considered quitting, but in a last-ditch marketing effort, they took some to Randolph Hodgson of Neal's Yard Dairy, a London retailer and exporter. Hodgson immediately recognized the superiority of Appleby's Cheshire and began vigorously promoting it.

Today, the Applebys' son and grandson carry on the work of the farm, overseeing the production of the only raw-milk, farmstead, cloth-bound Cheshire left in Britain. More than most other cheeses, Cheshire suffers from fast-paced mechanical processing. Only traditional hand methods produce the moist yet flaky texture and tangy acidity that define this cheese.

The Applebys make Cheshire in a wide range of sizes, but the eighteen-pound drum is most common in the United States. The wheels are aged for three to six months in their cloth wrap, which allows them to breathe and develop a natural rind. The pale pumpkin color of the paste derives from annatto, a harmless vegetable dye. The texture, though reminiscent of Cheddar, is moister and crumblier.

WINES THAT WORK: *A German Riesling Spätlese Trocken pairs body with racy acidity, just what this full-flavored, high-acid cheese needs. A red wine with some tannin and youthful fruit, such as a young Zinfandel or Cabernet Sauvignon, is pleasing as well.*

ASIAGO

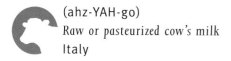

(ahz-YAH-go)
Raw or pasteurized cow's milk
Italy

Whether you prefer your cheese moist and mild or firm and bold, there is an Asiago for you. Italy's producers craft the cheese in a range of styles and ages, from twenty days to two years old. The more traditional cheese, Asiago d'Allevo, meaning "raised" or aged, has been made in the high plains of the Veneto for centuries. Fresh Asiago is a modern cheese, created to suit those who prefer more delicate tastes.

In the old days, Asiago d'Allevo was the product of two milkings. Cheesemakers would let the evening milk stand overnight so the cream would rise. The next day, they would skim the milk, combine it with the whole milk from the morning's milking, and proceed with cheesemaking. The result was a part-skim cheese capable of long aging. That practice continues today in traditional operations, but other producers now use modern skimming methods and make the cheese with only one milking. Fresh Asiago, in contrast, is always made with whole milk.

The mature wheels weigh about twenty pounds, the fresh wheels a little more. The younger cheese is smooth and mild, with the aroma of sweet milk and fresh grass and a tart finish. The mature cheeses range in age from *mezzano* (three to five months) to *vecchio* (nine months or more) to *stravecchio*, a hard cheese suitable for grating. At medium maturity, they are butter colored inside, with a semifirm paste that dissolves smoothly on the tongue, leaving a tangy, high-acid impression. Expect fruity and nutty aromas, with hints of caramel and grass.

WINES THAT WORK: *Light-bodied white wines, such as Pinot Grigio or Tocai Friulano, complement fresh Asiago. With a more mature Asiago, look to a medium- to full-bodied red wine, such as Chianti, Dolcetto d'Alba, Merlot, or Syrah.*

BAYLEY HAZEN BLUE

Jasper Hill Farm
Raw cow's milk
Vermont

Brothers Mateo and Andy Kehler bought a derelict Vermont farm in 1998, in an area that was losing dairy farms every year. The brothers hoped to create a new model for small-scale family farming, and they settled on cheesemaking as a way to add value to their milk. They now make three cheeses at Jasper Hill Farm, from the milk of about three dozen cows, but Bayley Hazen Blue (pictured on page 2) is perhaps their most acclaimed creation.

A tall, seven-pound cylinder that resembles Fourme d'Ambert (page 68), Bayley Hazen Blue is made year-round. Between May and September, the cows graze on pasture; the rest of the year, they spend in the barn, dining on local hay. The indoor diet produces more consistent cheese, the brothers say, but the summer wheels are capable of greater heights.

To produce the cheese, the fresh milk is cultured and inoculated with *Penicillium roqueforti*. Once the curds coalesce, they are scooped into forms that will yield a cheese about six inches wide and eight inches tall. After draining, they are unmolded and salted. At this early stage, the cheeses are white throughout. But the following week, they are pierced with needles to introduce the air that will prompt the blue mold to grow.

Bayley Hazen Blue is released after seventy-five to ninety days. By then, it has developed a natural rind dusted with powdery white molds. Inside, the ivory paste is rippled with well-spaced, blue-green veins. The texture is creamy yet crumbly, a little drier than most blue cheeses. The aroma can be baconlike, with hints of smoke and meat. The flavor is mellow, sweet, and approachable, without the bite of many blues.

WINES THAT WORK: *Choose a dessert wine with concentration and depth, such as Banyuls, Muscat de Rivesaltes, or tawny port.*

BEAUFORT

(BOW-fore)
Raw cow's milk
France

Fashioned into wheels weighing anywhere from forty-five to one hundred and fifty pounds, Beaufort belongs to the esteemed family of hefty cow's milk cheeses—Gruyère (page 77) and Comté (page 52) among them—made in the mountains between France and Switzerland. Its size reflects the realities of a cowherd's life in the Alps in pre-refrigeration days. Because cheesemakers pasturing their animals at high elevations could not easily send their products to the valley markets, they had to devise cheeses that would last until they came down from the mountain. Hence, the enormity of some of these traditional cheeses: big wheels age slowly.

Most Beaufort is made in cooperatives from the combined milk of several herds. Particularly prized is Beaufort d'été (summer Beaufort), which has a more golden color, generous aroma, and deeper flavor than winter Beaufort, all purportedly due to the varied diet of pastured animals. If the cheese has deep color and a roasted hazelnut and buttered-toast fragrance that you can't stop admiring, it is probably a summer cheese.

Like Abondance (page 26), Beaufort has convex sides, the result of tightening the strap that encircles the mold. Wheels mature for at least five months and for as long as a year, their interiors becoming progressively darker—from ivory to pale gold—and more aromatic with time.

Inside the hard rind, you will find a smooth, firm paste, which may glisten with fat at room temperature. Beaufort should be velvety, with perhaps a few tiny protein crystals and mingled aromas of fruit, brown butter, roasted meats, and nuts. Because the flavor is so concentrated, consider shaving Beaufort with a cheese plane and letting the slices melt on your tongue.

WINES THAT WORK: *Beaufort's sweet finish and creamy texture call for white wines with some viscosity. Many styles can work. Dry or off-dry amontillado sherry echoes the cheese's nutty notes. Other options include Alsatian Pinot Gris or Riesling, Grüner Veltliner, a creamy Chardonnay, or an off-dry Vouvray.*

BERKSWELL

Raw sheep's milk
England

Ram Hall, a sixteenth-century farmhouse in Coventry, has been in Stephen Fletcher's family for six generations. Fletcher doesn't know exactly how long the property has been farmed, but certainly for centuries. In the late 1980s, he redirected farm operations from cows to sheep and from fluid milk to cheese. By the mid-1990s, he was producing the award-winning Berkswell, which has helped to lead the British artisanal cheese renaissance.

Made initially with a recipe for Caerphilly, a British cow's milk cheese, Berkswell has departed from that model, evolving into a cheese that more closely resembles the sheep's milk cheeses of the French Pyrenees, such as Ossau-Iraty (page 101). Fletcher's wife, Tessa, now makes Berkswell using milk exclusively from the family's ewes. The sheep are on pasture from mid-April to late autumn, dining on the varied herbs and grasses that will flavor their milk.

A wheel of Berkswell weighs about six pounds and has an unusual bumpy surface thanks to the colander-like mold used to drain the curds. Aging lasts for four to eight months, with the cheese becoming progressively drier and more intensely flavored. At medium maturity, the paste will be golden and firm, with a dense, silky texture not unlike that of Gruyère. At room temperature, droplets of fat may appear on the surface, a reminder of the exceptional richness of sheep's milk. The aroma is of caramel and brown butter, while the finish is balanced, sweet, tangy, and lingering.

WINES THAT WORK: *A medium- to full-bodied red wine without strong tannins, such as Syrah or Australian Shiraz, matches Berkswell in flavor intensity. Or complement its caramel scent with a gently sweet fortified wine, such as amontillado sherry or Madeira.*

BLEU D'AUVERGNE

(bleu do-VER-nyeh)
Raw (rare) or pasteurized cow's milk
France

Perhaps the most famous French blue cheese after Roquefort, Bleu d'Auvergne is creamier, less salty, and generally less pungent than its better-known neighbor. Made in the mountainous Auvergne region of south-central France and weighing five to six pounds, the wheels have a natural rind with a dusting of powdery white molds. The ivory interior shows generous blue-gray veining.

Bleu d'Auvergne dates from the 1850s, the creation of Antoine Roussel, a young cheesemaker who noticed that his cave-aged cheeses were developing blue veins spontaneously. Roussel liked the character that the blue added and began experimenting with ways to encourage the veins to grow. After realizing that rye bread often developed the same sort of mold, he began inoculating his young cheeses with spores from the bread.

Apparently, Roussel also recognized that the mold needed air to grow, so he began piercing his cheeses to create air tunnels. Supplied with oxygen, the spores took off, creating rich veins of blue in the air pockets. Today, this technique of "needling" cheeses to introduce the oxygen the blue molds need to thrive is common practice.

Wheels of Bleu d'Auvergne mature for at least four weeks and often much longer, becoming more potent as they age. The flavor is robust, even spicy, but never overly piquant or sharp, and the texture is moist, dense, and buttery. Fresh figs or ripe pears are good partners.

WINES THAT WORK: *For a young and mild Bleu d'Auvergne, choose a wine with a touch of sweetness, such as an off-dry California Riesling or a German Riesling Kabinett. More mature and pungent cheeses call for a sweeter wine with more concentration, such as Sauternes, Banyuls, or tawny port.*

BOERENKAAS

(BOOR-en-kahss)
Raw cow's milk
The Netherlands

Literally "farmer's cheese," Boerenkaas is the traditional raw-milk, farm-made version of the waxed Gouda on most supermarket shelves. Gouda production in the Netherlands is largely industrialized now, but about three hundred and fifty farmers still produce this cheese by hand methods and give it the extended aging that develops character. On most of these farms, the time-honored roles persist: the women make the cheese because their husbands tend the cows and are too dirty to permit in the cheese room.

Boerenkaas wheels vary in size but generally weigh twenty-five to thirty-five pounds. They range in age from several months to several years—five-year-old specimens are not uncommon—but most wheels in the United States are twelve to twenty-four months old. To produce a cheese with such longevity, the cheesemaker must remove as much whey from the fresh curds as possible; high-moisture cheeses do not age. Cooking the curds in the cheese vat drives off whey, as does pressing the curds once they are molded—two steps essential to the production of aged Gouda.

When relatively young—say, under a year—Boerenkaas has a golden color and a smooth, dense, creamy texture, with subtle caramel notes. As the cheese matures, the color darkens, progressing to deep gold, then butterscotch. The texture becomes drier and harder and the flavors more concentrated, with both saltiness and sweetness intensified. A two- or three-year-old Boerenkaas can smell like whiskey and taste like butterscotch candy, a far cry from bland factory-made Gouda in its red wax coat.

WINES THAT WORK: *Complement the caramel aromas of Boerenkaas with a dry or off-dry amontillado sherry or Rainwater Madeira. Sparkling wine can also handle its salty intensity.*

Same Cheese, Different Source

Just as wine lovers often compare the same variety from different regions, cheese enthusiasts may find it enlightening to taste similar cheeses of different origins side by side. On this cheese board showcasing two of the world's finest Cheddars (page 51), California goes head-to-head with England. As you taste, note the similarities and the differences in color, texture, aroma, and depth of flavor. With a little experimenting, you may discover intriguing combinations for a party platter. See page 141 for a by-country listing of the cheeses profiled in this book.

Fiscalini Farmstead Bandage-Wrapped Cheddar

Montgomery's Cheddar

< TOP TO BOTTOM: Montgomery's Cheddar and Fiscalini Cheddar

BRIE

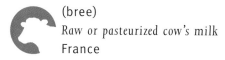

(bree)
Raw or pasteurized cow's milk
France

A perfect Brie, supple on the inside and redolent of mushrooms, is one of the great achievements of French cheesemaking. Unfortunately, Americans searching for that impeccably made and ripened cheese are much more likely to find it in France, despite the popularity of Brie in the United States. The finest Bries are made from raw milk, but the Food and Drug Administration does not permit importation of raw-milk Brie because it is too high in moisture and insufficiently aged to meet U.S. food-safety requirements. Nevertheless, American cheese counters sell truckloads of Brie, and some of it can be pretty good. It can also be bitter, salty, and ammoniated, so it always pays to ask for a taste before purchasing.

There is not one Brie, but several, all of them made in northeast France, east of Paris. Brie de Meaux and Brie de Melun both have AOC status (see page 142). Brie de Nangis (rare in the United States) and Brie de Coulommiers, also called simply Coulommiers, do not. Brie de Meaux is generally considered to be the king of Bries, but if you have a choice, buy on taste. An unripe Brie de Meaux will be inferior to a ripe Coulommiers.

To produce Brie's soft, moist, velvety texture, the curds are cut large and drained without pressing. *Penicillium candidum*—added to the milk or sprayed on the fresh wheels—produces the bloomy white exterior as the cheese matures. This mold is largely responsible for ripening Brie from the outside in. Some people prefer their cheese with a touch of firmness at the core; others like it soft all the way through. In any case, Brie should not be runny. When ripe, it will give to gentle pressure and have some reddish markings on its snowy rind.

WINES THAT WORK: *Brie needs a white wine with some texture, such as unoaked or lightly oaked Chardonnay or Pinot Gris. Red wines of medium body and moderate tannin, such as Syrah and Merlot, also fare well with Brie, and sparkling wine is particularly pleasing.*

BRILLAT-SAVARIN

(bree-yaht sah-vah-RIN)
Pasteurized cow's milk
France

With its fluffy, whipped cream texture and nutty, sour cream taste, Brillat-Savarin (pictured on page 2) has captivated consumers since its creation in the 1930s. The invention of Parisian cheese merchant Henri Androuët, Brillat-Savarin takes its name from the eighteenth-century French gastronome, Jean Anthelme Brillat-Savarin. This wise man memorably remarked that a day without cheese is like a beautiful woman with only one eye. In both cases, something is missing.

Brillat-Savarin is classified as a *triple-crème* cheese, indicating that the milk used in its production has been enriched with cream or, in the case of Brillat-Savarin, with tangy crème fraîche.

Made by several dairies in northern France, Brillat-Savarin comes to market only two to three weeks old, weighing a little over one pound. It has a bloomy white rind, the result of molds sprayed on the cheese early in its life and nurtured in the aging room. Some people prefer Brillat-Savarin when the rind is still snow-white. Others like it a little riper, when the rind develops some golden markings. Beware of specimens with sunken or well-mottled exteriors, signs they are overripe.

The interior of a ripe Brillat-Savarin will be pale ivory and as silky, smooth, and spreadable as cake frosting. It should have a faint cultured-milk smell, with no evident ammonia, and a gentle lactic tang, like cultured butter. The salt level is often elevated in Brillat-Savarin and other *triple-crème* cheeses, but it should not be so high that it interferes with enjoyment. Walnut bread is a lovely companion for this luscious dessert cheese.

WINES THAT WORK: *Champagne and other sparkling wines, always high in acid, provide a palate-cleansing contrast to the richness of the cheese. Or you can echo Brillat-Savarin's creamy texture with a lush Napa Valley Chardonnay.*

BRIN D'AMOUR

(brin dah-MOOR)
Raw sheep's milk
France

The mountainous island of Corsica supports sheep and goat dairying, with the animals grazing in season on the rocky shrubland known as maquis. This rugged landscape is blanketed with wild herbs in spring and summer, including the rosemary and savory that coat each small square of Brin d'Amour (sprig of love). Still made artisanally, the aromatic cheese also goes by the evocative name of Fleur du Maquis (flower of the maquis), although juniper berries are usually mixed with the herbs in a true Fleur du Maquis.

Brin d'Amour varies in size, but the largest is just over two pounds. The shape is round or roughly squarish, about two inches thick, with a bloomy rind dappled with gray mold underneath the blanket of herbs. The cheeses are matured for one to three months, becoming firmer and more herbaceous as they age. Young specimens are moist, tender, and smooth, with a texture resembling firm tofu and a decidedly lemony finish. The herbs perfume the interior without obscuring the flavor of the sheep's milk. You will want to trim the rind away as you eat—the herbs are coarse and twiggy— but underneath, you will find a smooth, ivory cheese imbued with the scent of the Corsican countryside.

WINES THAT WORK: *Pour a Sauvignon Blanc, Vermentino, or dry rosé if the cheese is moist, young, and lemony. With firmer, more herbaceous cheeses, move to a full-bodied white, such as Viognier or Marsanne, or a light- to medium-bodied red, such as a Grenache or Merlot.*

CAMELLIA

Redwood Hill Farm
Pasteurized goat's milk
California

When Jennifer Bice took over her parents' Sonoma County goat dairy in the late 1970s, goat cheese was still a rarity on American tables. Bice sold her raw goat's milk to health- and natural-food stores and gradually added yogurt to her line to extend the milk's shelf life. But by the early 1990s, many of Bice's customers were asking her for goat cheese. She now makes a range of them, including goat Feta, goat Cheddar, and the Camembert-like Camellia.

Weighing only four ounces, the petite, round Camellia makes a generous cheese course for two or enough for four with other selections. Like Camembert, its inspiration, it is a mold-ripened cheese. In other words, the surface molds do much of the work of breaking down the milk proteins and softening the cheese from the outside in.

Bice says that Camellia's quality peaks in winter, when the goats' milk is higher in solids and butterfat. The cheese matures more predictably then, becoming creamy and runny after six to eight weeks of ripening. Large-scale cheese producers often standardize their milk to the same fat and protein content year-round, so their recipes never change. Cheese artisans like Bice must adapt their recipes to accommodate seasonal changes in the milk.

When Camellia gives to gentle pressure in the center, it is ready to eat. It should have a pristine bloomy rind. Significant tan mottling is an indication that the surface molds are dying and the cheese may be ammoniated. Inside, the pale paste should be soft and oozy, calling out for a slice of baguette or toast. The taste will be mild and uncomplicated, with the recognizable flavor of goat's milk.

WINES THAT WORK: *Full-bodied dry whites with no appreciable oak are a nice textural match for this delicate, creamy cheese. Look to Chardonnay or white Burgundy, Pinot Gris, Bordeaux Blanc, Viognier, or German Riesling Spätlese Trocken. Pinot Noir also works, but a bigger red will overwhelm it.*

CAMEMBERT

(cam-om-BEAR)
Pasteurized cow's milk
France

The Camembert sold in the United States is not the beloved Camembert de Normandie, an AOC cheese (see page 142) that must, by regulation, be made with raw milk. You will have to go to France to taste that. The U.S. government does not allow the importation of raw-milk cheeses aged less than sixty days, as Camembert de Normandie is. So we must settle for variations of Camembert made with pasteurized milk.

At its best, imported Camembert has mushroom aromas and a supple, seductive texture. It should finish without bitterness or strong ammoniated character. Some people like the cheese when it is verging on runny. Others prefer it when it is still a little firm at the core. It ripens from the outside in, so you can estimate its readiness by gently pressing the surface. The degree of resistance will tell you whether it has reached the stage you like. The state of the rind provides another clue, as it develops some golden or reddish stippling as the cheese ages. The more marking, the riper the cheese.

To achieve the silky, moist interior characteristic of fine Camembert, the fresh curds must be handled gently. They are hand-ladled into their molds at the best dairies, and they drain only from their own weight; they are never pressed. When they are firm enough to unmold, they are sprayed with the spores that will, over a period of about three weeks, enrobe the nine-ounce disks with a velvety white coat.

Should you eat the Camembert rind? That is a matter of taste. If it is not ammoniated and you like the contrast of textures, by all means eat it. If it is strong or diminishes your pleasure, cut it away. Both approaches are correct.

WINES THAT WORK: *With a flavor and texture almost identical to Brie, Camembert calls for a similar wine choice (see page 138). A buttery Chardonnay without obvious oak makes an appealing match, as does sparkling wine or a Grüner Veltliner at the richer end of its spectrum. For a red, choose a medium-weight wine with modest tannin, such as Merlot.*

CANTAL

(cahn-TAHL)
Raw or pasteurized cow's milk
France

One of France's most ancient cheeses, Cantal hails from the Auvergne, source of many of the country's finest cheeses. A large cylinder weighing eighty to ninety pounds, Cantal owes its depth of flavor and creamy texture to an unusual manufacturing process similar to that used for Cheddar.

Once the milk is cultured and rennet is added, the resulting curds are gathered and mechanically pressed into a slab. The slab is cut by hand, then pressed a second time. Finally, the slab is ground into small bits, salted, and packed into tall, cloth-lined molds, at which point it undergoes yet another pressing. All this cutting and pressing compacts the curd and expels moisture, resulting in a wheel that is capable of long aging. Rest periods between the pressings allow the curd to develop lactic acid, notable in the finished cheese.

After one to two months of aging (the legal minimum is one month), Cantal is moist and mild, with a pale interior and a lactic aroma. But the cheese develops much more personality with age. At six months, it is known as *vieux* (mature) Cantal and has a smooth, butter-colored interior, possibly with some cracks, and a buff-colored natural rind stained with red and white molds. The aroma of these older wheels suggests buttermilk or sour cream; the flavor is tangy yet balanced and holds your attention for taste after taste.

Although sightings are rare in the United States, keep your eyes out for Salers. Another product of the Auvergne, it is a virtual twin to Cantal but always made with raw milk.

WINES THAT WORK: *Select a rich white, such as an Alsatian Pinot Gris, or a Beaujolais or Pinot Noir. The more mature and full-flavored the cheese, the bigger the wine should be.*

CASHEL BLUE

Pasteurized cow's milk
Ireland

Louis and Jane Grubb began making cheese in the early 1980s, using the milk of their own herd. Today, many consider their cheese to be Ireland's finest blue. The cows are on pasture from April to October in County Tipperary, and the Grubbs are convinced of the superiority of this summer milk. Given that aging lasts at least three months, with four to five months even better, the finest wheels reach the market in late autumn and winter.

The milk for Cashel Blue (pictured on page 16) is inoculated with *Penicillium roqueforti*, the same mold used to make the famous French blue. The mold lies dormant until the wheels are pierced on about day four. Over the following two weeks, the veins will spread internally, working their way into the air pockets in this moist, unpressed cheese. When the cheesemaker determines that the veining is sufficient, the wheels are wrapped in foil to halt the blueing. Then they spend at least three months in a cool aging room, becoming creamier and more mellow. Neal's Yard Dairy, a London exporter, ages the wheels further before shipping them to the United States, but not all exporters do.

Louis Grubb compares the maturation of his cheeses to the slow development of teenagers. Cashel Blue is flaky, sharp, and acidic when young, he says, but with maturity comes creaminess, complexity, and a more subdued character.

A three- to four-pound cylinder of Cashel Blue has a beautiful appearance, with well-spaced blue-gray veins in an ivory background. The texture is moister and creamier than many blues, with restrained salt and an ingratiating butteriness. If the cheese "weeps" at room temperature, pat it dry with a paper towel.

WINES THAT WORK: *Sparkling wine will contrast nicely with the cheese's creaminess, while an amontillado sherry will complement its mellow character. A botrytised dessert wine, such as Sauternes or late-harvest Riesling, will also work, as long as it is not syrupy sweet.*

CHEDDAR

Raw or pasteurized cow's milk
England and United States

Cheddar's reputation has suffered in the United States due to the tasteless, waxy blocks of rindless cheese sold under that name in most supermarkets. Traditional cloth-bound Cheddar is one of the most complex and captivating cheeses made anywhere. England still can claim a handful of raw-milk farmhouse Cheddars, such as Montgomery's (pictured on page 38), Keen's, Quicke's, and Westcombe. The United States can boast of the excellent Cheddar made by Fiscalini Farms in California (see photos pages 23, 38, 140) and Shelburne Farms and Grafton Village in Vermont. What makers of these fine Cheddars have in common is their use of the so-called cheddaring process and their commitment to long, slow aging.

To make Cheddar, the drained curds are gathered into large slabs at the side of the cheese vat, then the slabs are stacked by hand two or three high and repeatedly turned. The cheesemaker controls the loss of whey and the development of acid by the height of the stack. When the acidity is correct, the curds are milled and packed in cheesecloth-lined molds. The wheels are pressed to tighten the texture, then unmolded and sent to an aging room for a stay that may last from nine months to two years.

Grafton Village departs from this process by aging its cheeses in blocks in plastic bags. The blocks never develop the natural rind of cloth-bound Cheddar, and they age more slowly—Grafton Cheddars can be five years old—but the results are excellent.

Good Cheddar has a firm texture that manages to be simultaneously crumbly yet creamy. The acidity is pronounced and the aromas are profound: grassy, fruity, and nutty, often with caramel notes. As a morsel dissolves on the tongue, it leaves a balanced impression, mingling saltiness, sweetness, and acidity, and the flavors linger long after the morsel is gone.

WINES THAT WORK: *You need a red wine with some intensity to stand up to Cheddar. Zinfandel, Merlot, Cabernet Sauvignon, and Bordeaux typically have the richness that the cheese needs. Alternatively, consider a dry amontillado sherry or an off-dry oloroso sherry, both beautiful matches.*

COMTÉ

(CON-tay)
Raw cow's milk
France

Made in the Jura Mountains of eastern France, Comté is one of that country's best-selling cheeses. The milk must come from Montbéliard cows that have access to plentiful pasture. And before any wheels can be sold as Comté, they must pass an evaluation by a panel of experts. Specimens receiving less than twelve points on a twenty-point scale are denied the Comté label; those scoring fifteen points or more receive a special green stamp.

Few farmers have enough cows to make an eighty-pound wheel of Comté every day, so the cheese is largely made in cooperative dairies. There are about two hundred of these dairies in the region, working with milk from more than three thousand farms. After coagulation in big copper vats, the fresh curds are heated to firm them and drive off whey. Once molded, the wheels are pressed to expel more moisture and yield the firm, tight texture and aging potential expected of Comté.

After a few weeks of curing at the dairy, the wheels are transferred to aging cellars, where they remain for a minimum of four or as long as twenty-four months. During their stay, they receive regular sponge baths with bacteria-laced brine to sustain the rind and develop flavor.

Age concentrates the flavor and deepens the color of Comté. The interior may be ivory if made from winter milk, or more yellow if made in summer from cows that dined on carotene-rich pasture. With age, the color darkens to gold and the aromas of hazelnut and brown butter intensify. At any age, the texture will be smooth, never granular, and the flavors will be impeccably balanced between sweet, salty, and tart.

WINES THAT WORK: *Look to the rich, spicy white wines from Alsace, such as Pinot Gris or Riesling, or to an off-dry Vouvray or dry amontillado sherry. Chardonnay with a creamy texture but without obvious oak is another good choice.*

CRESCENZA

(creh-SHEN-za)
Bellwether Farms
Pasteurized cow's milk
California

Modeled after a fresh cheese of the same name from northern Italy, Bellwether Farms's Crescenza is less than a week old when it leaves the dairy. Soft, sweet, milky, and mild, it is only a few steps removed from fresh milk.

Cheesemaker Liam Callahan traveled to Italy to master the method for this cheese, also known in Italy as Stracchino. The technique requires extrarich milk, which Callahan obtains from local Jersey cows. After culturing and coagulating the milk, he cuts the curds large to avoid losing too much whey. If cut smaller, they would expel too much moisture and the finished cheese would be too dry.

The fresh curds are gently ladled into square molds large enough to make an inch-thick cheese that weighs two to three pounds. After a day's draining, the cheese is firm enough to unmold. It spends an hour in a brine bath, which seasons it, and then a couple of days in a drying room. At that point, the big, floppy squares are packaged in plastic to prevent leakage—they are still quite moist and drippy—and shipped.

You cannot expect a fresh cheese like Crescenza to have the complexity of an aged cheese. What it offers instead is a soft, yielding texture; a gentle, cultured-milk tartness, like sour cream; and the pure, direct sweetness of Jersey milk. Many of its fans enjoy it melted on pizza or polenta. Some prefer it as a breakfast cheese with fruit, or spread on walnut bread. It is also delicious drizzled with extra virgin olive oil, sprinkled with sea salt and cracked black pepper, and served with a green salad.

WINES THAT WORK: *A dry rosé or a fresh, light, crisp white wine, such as Pinot Grigio or dry Riesling, is the best companion for this fresh, tart cheese.*

DRY MONTEREY JACK

Vella Cheese Company
Pasteurized cow's milk
California

During World War I, when supplies of authentic Italian Parmigiano-Reggiano disappeared, Americans turned to Dry Jack for a substitute. The cheese wholesalers around San Francisco had already figured out that you could produce a respectable grating cheese by salting wheels of fresh, mild California Jack and putting them away for months. With Parmigiano-Reggiano unavailable, sales of Dry Jack soared.

For decades following the war, California boasted numerous Dry Jack producers. Now only a handful remain, with Vella Cheese Company, in downtown Sonoma, the acknowledged king. Cheesemaker Ig Vella pioneered America's artisanal cheese movement and has mentored many others. His flagship Dry Jack is widely esteemed.

The eight-pound wheels are shaped laboriously by hand. Workers gather the curds in muslin bags, roll the bags against the sides of the cheese vat until they are round, and then tie the bags with string and press them overnight. On a whole wheel, you can spot the impressions made by the bag and the "navel" where the string was tied.

Ig Vella's father, Tom, concocted the cheese's unusual coating: vegetable oil, which keeps it from cracking as it dries, mixed with cocoa and black pepper, which prevent the oil from seeping in. After seven to eight months, the wheels have a hard, powdery, cocoa-colored rind unique in the cheese world.

An eight-month-old Dry Jack has a firm, waxy golden paste with a subtle nutty aroma and expertly balanced sweetness, saltiness, and acidity. Wheels aged for a year or more are tagged Special Select; they become drier, smoother, and a little nuttier, although eventually there are diminishing returns. Vella himself likes his Dry Jack best at about sixteen months. Beyond that, he says, the cheese just gets harder, not better.

WINES THAT WORK: *Most wines, red and white, can happily accompany Vella Dry Jack. Indeed, it is almost hard to arrange a bad match. But for the pleasure of enjoying a wine and a cheese from the same region, pour a Zinfandel from Sonoma County's Dry Creek Valley.*

American All-Stars

The diversity of American artisanal cheesemaking is on display on this cheese board, featuring three unique creations, all made on a small scale.

California's Redwood Hill Farm produces the goat's milk Camellia (page 45).

From Oregon comes the cow's milk Rogue River Blue (page 118) wrapped in grape leaves. The Matos family makes the cow's milk St. George (page 124).

Together, this trio makes a powerful case for the sophistication of modern American cheeses. (See page 141 for a list of U.S.-made cheeses included in this book.)

Camellia

Rogue River Blue

St. George

< CLOCKWISE FROM TOP LEFT: *Rogue River Blue, St. George, and Camellia*

DURRUS

Raw cow's milk
Ireland

Traditional farmhouse cheese production had all but died in Ireland when Jeffa Gill bought her farm in rural County Cork in the mid-1970s. A former Dublin fashion designer, Gill initially planned to grow and sell organic vegetables, but the demand didn't materialize. So she switched to cheese, first experimenting on her kitchen stove with the milk of her eight cows. In 1979, she launched the washed-rind Durrus, named for her village, and is now considered a pioneer in the revitalization of Irish artisanal cheesemaking.

Gill eventually sold her cows to focus on the cheese. She now buys her milk from a neighbor and transforms it into wheels of two sizes: about fourteen ounces and a little over three pounds. The cheese is made in a copper vat, and the curds are cut by hand with a cheese harp, an implement that resembles a giant comb. The freshly formed wheels are brined briefly before moving into a curing room, where they will spend a minimum of three to five weeks, with frequent turning and washing. Over time, the moist rind attracts desirable bacteria, which turn the surface a pinkish orange and imbue the cheese with enticing aromas.

In Ireland, the cheese is marketed at this early age, when the interior is supple and the rind still moist and sticky. But because the cheese is made from raw milk, it must be aged at least sixty days to enter the United States, so the Durrus sold in this country is two to three months old. The rind is dry and may be orange to brown and powdered with white mold. The semisoft paste will be a deep gold with many small eyes, and the fragrance will fill a room with the mingled aromas of Brazil nuts, earth, and bread yeast.

WINES THAT WORK: *Durrus needs a wine of pronounced character to match its intensity. Pour a Syrah, the cheesemaker's favorite companion, or a Gewürztraminer.*

L'ÉDEL DE CLÉRON

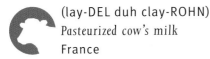

(lay-DEL duh clay-ROHN)
Pasteurized cow's milk
France

Before the U.S. government became more vigilant in keeping out underage raw-milk cheeses, consumers could experience the pleasure of an authentic French or Swiss Vacherin Mont d'Or. With those cheeses no longer available, we must be content with second best, the luscious L'Édel de Cléron (pictured on pages 11, 23), made in imitation of Vacherin but from pasteurized milk.

From the Franche-Comté, source of the giant Comté cheeses, L'Édel de Cléron is made in two sizes: a petite round weighing about seven ounces and a larger one of about four and a half pounds. Traditionally, the local farmers made small cheeses such as these when the winter weather turned fierce and they couldn't get their milk to the cooperative dairy. L'Édel de Cléron is made year-round, but many still associate it with cold-weather dining. In rural homes in France's Jura Mountains, it might be the centerpiece of a winter meal with boiled potatoes, white wine, and some fruit for dessert.

Making L'Édel de Cléron, sometimes called faux Vacherin, is a painstaking process. The rounds must be encircled with a strip of spruce bark to guard against the cheese collapsing when ripe. Over the month or so of their maturation, the disks are repeatedly washed with brine to encourage the growth of desirable bacteria on the surface. As the cheese ripens, the rind develops a crusty and rippled appearance. If perfectly ripe, L'Édel de Cléron can be molten enough to eat with a spoon, but retailers tend to sell the cheese younger than that.

Most likely, the texture will be oozy but still sliceable, the fragrance redolent of mushrooms and earth. Near the retaining wall of the bark, the aroma becomes more woodsy and resinlike, a pleasing perfume, though not as heady as the truffled scent of a Vacherin.

WINES THAT WORK: *Pinot Noir complements the cheese aromatically. An Alsatian Pinot Gris or Riesling should also have the weight and intensity to partner this fragrant cheese.*

ÉPOISSES

(ay-PWAHSS)
Pasteurized cow's milk
France

A centuries-old cheese named for its Burgundy birthplace, Époisses is one of several washed-rind cheeses with monastery origins. Some say that monks excelled at making the meaty, washed-rind cheeses because they had to abstain from meat so often.

Époisses derives some of its character from its especially slow coagulation of sixteen hours or more. This leisurely fermentation allows for the gradual development of lactic acid, which eventually causes curds to form. (Most other cheeses rely on rennet or other enzymes to produce the same result far more quickly.)

Hand-ladling the curds into their molds helps produce Époisses's voluptuous texture. The cheese's pungent aroma develops later, the result of the washing. Repeatedly during their five- to eight-week maturation, the wheels are sponged with water mixed with Marc de Bourgogne, the local brandy. The moist surface invites the growth of desirable bacteria that eventually give the mature cheese a reddish orange exterior and a potent perfume.

A ripe Époisses smells of mushrooms, meat, and garlic. Under the sticky orange rind, the ivory interior should be soft and supple and just shy of molten. Like most washed-rind cheeses, Époisses is milder than its fragrance would suggest. Do eat the crunchy rind, a pleasing contrast to the creamy interior.

Despite its long history, Époisses all but disappeared following World War II. The Berthaut family revived the cheese in the 1950s, and the Berthaut firm is still considered one of the best producers. Époisses is made in two sizes—the smaller about eight ounces, the larger a little over two pounds—but many retailers carry only the smaller version, as it is easier to handle.

WINES THAT WORK: *A dry Pinot Gris or Riesling from Alsace has the intensity to stand up to an aromatic Époisses. Many people enjoy it with red Burgundy, but the cheese can overwhelm the wine. Proceed with caution.*

L'ÉTIVAZ

(lay-tee-VAHZ)
Raw cow's milk
Switzerland

Switzerland's first AOC cheese (see page 142), a status awarded in 2000, L'Étivaz merits the honor. The strict rules governing its production state that it can only be made between May 10 and October 10, from the raw milk of cows grazing between one thousand and two thousand meters (three thousand and six thousand feet) in a restricted zone of the Swiss Alps. Eighty families tend the herds on this lush high-mountain pasture. They take the milk to one of one hundred and thirty *chalets d'alpage* (mountain huts), where it is cooked in large cauldrons over a wood fire and transformed into curds.

Few AOC regulations are as specific and demanding as those for L'Étivaz. They require that the curds be cut by hand, not mechanically, and that they be lifted from the cauldron in large cloth or nylon bags and molded by hand, practices that have long vanished from many cheese plants. After a week, the young wheels are transported to large cooperative aging facilities where they are matured on spruce shelves for at least four and a half months. Skilled *affineurs* (cheese agers) turn them frequently and rub them with brine to nurture the rind, a considerable labor for wheels that may weigh up to eighty pounds.

The cheesemakers claim that the wheels are not fully mature until eight months, and that some will continue to improve for up to a year. With these firm mountain cheeses, time intensifies everything: the color, the aroma, the taste. If you like Gruyère, you will love L'Étivaz, which seems to have all of Gruyère's attributes and then some. The paste is dense, smooth, and silky, with aromas of smoke and hazelnuts and the rich, oily, lingering flavor of Brazil nuts.

WINES THAT WORK: *The concentrated flavors of L'Étivaz call for an intense white wine, such as a Pinot Gris or Pinot Blanc from Alsace or Oregon, a Grüner Veltliner at the rich end of its spectrum, or German Riesling Spätlese.*

FETA

(FEH-ta)
Pasteurized sheep's or mixed sheep's and goat's milk
Greece

Salty, moist, and tangy, Feta adds a spark to summer salads of tomato, greens, and cucumber. Mild and creamy when young, it becomes more peppery and complex with age, ideal for pairing with beets or roasted peppers, or for dressing with olive oil and dried oregano.

By Greek law, Feta must contain a minimum of 70 percent sheep's milk, which contributes richness and creaminess, with the remainder goat's milk. Most Greek farmers have mixed herds, and the proportion of sheep's to goat's milk the herd yields varies with the seasons.

To make Feta, slabs of fresh cheese are layered with salt for a day or more. The salt flavors the cheese and draws moisture out of it. After this initial seasoning, the slabs are rinsed and packed into barrels (the traditional way) or into sealed tins (the modern way). In this environment, they will exude their own brine and mature for several more weeks. Minimum age is two months, but barrel-aged Feta can be matured for up to a year and will only improve.

Feta should be white or off-white, with a moist and creamy yet crumbly texture, a pronounced but not excessive saltiness, and a pleasant sour tang. It should not be grainy. The word *feta* means "slice," typically the form in which it is served. Try to buy it from a store that keeps it in its brine, which helps preserve it. If it has no brine, you can make one at home by dissolving one-quarter cup of sea salt in one quart water.

Bulgaria and France also make good Feta. The Bulgarian style is tangier, the French milder and creamier. Feta produced in most other countries rarely measures up.

WINES THAT WORK: *Lean white wines, such as Sauvignon Blanc and Pinot Grigio, or dry rosés are the best match for Feta's tangy saltiness.*

FONTINA

(fon-TEE-na)
Raw cow's milk
Italy

The best time to purchase Fontina is in the late fall, when merchants have wheels made from the milk of cows that grazed on summer pasture. The aromatic herbs, wildflowers, and grasses of the Valle d'Aosta, a mountainous region of northwest Italy, nourish the cows in summer, yielding particularly fine milk for cheesemaking. A wheel made in June will be superb by October.

Making cheese is an age-old practice in these rugged mountains, which are better suited to livestock than crops. The DOP regulations (see page 142) for Fontina do not allow the mixing of morning and evening milks, so cheesemakers must repeat their procedures twice a day.

Young wheels of Fontina are repeatedly washed with brine to develop the rind, then matured in natural caves for three to four months. Before the wheels receive final approval, an inspector takes a small, pluglike sample and attempts to bend it. If the two ends touch, the cheese has the proper supple texture.

Fontina has a firm, golden rind and a compact, straw-colored interior with a few small holes. The wheels are three to four inches tall and weigh eighteen to forty pounds, with the heavier wheels bigger in diameter rather than thicker. The aroma is nutty and faintly herbaceous, the texture smooth, and the finish sweet. Fontina melts beautifully and is used in many regional dishes, including polenta and the fonduelike *fonduta* with shaved truffles.

WINES THAT WORK: *Look to white wines with richness and body to complement Fontina's earthy notes and touch of sweetness. Alsatian Pinot Gris, Viognier, and California or French Chardonnay that is not overtly fruity are all harmonious. Red wines without a lot of tannin, such as Pinot Noir or Syrah, will work, too. Or pour a dry amontillado sherry to echo Fontina's nutty notes.*

FOURME D'AMBERT

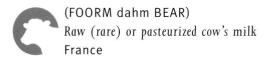

(FOORM dahm BEAR)
Raw (rare) or pasteurized cow's milk
France

For centuries, the people in the surrounding countryside sold their *fourmes* (an archaic French word for cheeses) in Ambert, a small town in the Auvergne. At one time, the blue-veined Fourme d'Ambert was even part of the peasants' annual tithe to the church. It is particularly eye-catching, a cylinder half again as tall as it is wide and weighing about five pounds. Traditionally, it is cut horizontally to make a round for the cheese board. Diners then cut wedges from the round.

In the old days, production was almost entirely on the farm and from raw milk. Today, most Fourme d'Ambert is made in large dairies from pasteurized milk, and connoisseurs bemoan the loss in quality.

The milk is inoculated with the same mold spores used to make the more famous Roquefort. When the cheeses are only two to three days old, still perfectly white and nearly flavorless, they are pierced to make air channels. The sleepy mold spores then spring into action, creating the blue veins that give the cheese its character.

Minimum age is twenty-eight days, but the best producers age their wheels for two to three months. During that time, the cheese develops a natural rind splotched with white and reddish molds. Inside, the ivory paste becomes liberally laced with blue-gray veins and develops a delightful creaminess. Well-made Fourme d'Ambert delivers mouthfilling flavor without being pungent, salty, or bitter.

WINES THAT WORK: *Choose a dessert wine to balance this cheese's salt and mold, but because the cheese is relatively mild, the wine need not be supersweet. A young Sauternes, Barsac, Bergerac, or Coteaux du Layon will complement this cheese and keep the theme within France.*

GARROTXA

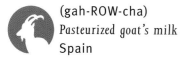

(gah-ROW-cha)
Pasteurized goat's milk
Spain

In the late 1980s, a cooperative of goat farmers in the Garrotxa area of Catalonia revived an indigenous local cheese that had all but disappeared. The members were urban refugees, back-to-the-landers who had fled city jobs in favor of rural life. They had education and technical skills, and they directed their talents to cheesemaking.

The happy result is Garrotxa (pictured on page 74), a semiaged goat cheese with a sweet, nutty flavor and a downy, mold-covered rind. The wheels are small, about three pounds, and need only a few weeks in the humid environment of the Pyrenees to develop naturally a bluish gray bloom on the surface. Typical maturation is six to eight weeks.

Inside is a dense, smooth, ivory paste that melts on the tongue. Garrotxa has the sweet, cooked-milk notes of Gruyère but a more buttery texture. The *Penicillium* molds on the rind impart a faint blue-cheese flavor that might fool you if you tasted the cheese with your eyes closed.

There are now many producers of Garrotxa spread all over Catalonia. The recipe is not standardized, so you can expect some variation.

WINES THAT WORK: *The best white wines for Garrotxa are neither too austere nor too sweet. Pinot Gris, Verdejo, and Chardonnay will work if they have some texture to complement the cheese's buttery sweetness. Or pour fino or dry amontillado sherry to bring out Garroxta's nuttiness.*

GORGONZOLA

(gor-gon-ZO-lah)
Pasteurized cow's milk
Italy

Italy's most famous blue cheese (pictured on page 19) comes from the Lombardy and Piedmont regions in the northern part of the country. It is centuries old, although production methods have been modernized. In the past, the cheese developed its blue veins naturally. The cheesemaker would coagulate the evening milk and leave the curd out overnight to become impregnated with ambient molds before adding the morning milk to it.

Today's cheesemakers don't leave the mold development to chance. They inoculate the milk with the *Penicillium* strains they want. The mold spores lie in wait until the still-white wheels are pierced with stainless-steel needles at three to four weeks of age. The influx of air awakens the molds, and they begin to proliferate in the air channels.

Gorgonzola *dolce* ("sweet" Gorgonzola) is ready for market in two months. It is notably creamy and mild, with a luscious texture that compensates for its lack of complexity. Gorgonzola *naturale*, sometimes called mountain Gorgonzola, delivers more character. Made with a different culture than the *dolce* and matured for three to six months, it becomes increasingly firm and spicy, with a penetrating flavor and more veining.

About sixty different producers—some large, some small—make Gorgonzola, so quality can vary. Look for wheels with evenly spaced veining and a flavor that is not excessively hot, salty, or bitter. Like many other blue cheeses, Gorgonzola is foil wrapped to prevent drying and to halt the blue-mold growth.

WINES THAT WORK: *Sparkling wine provides an appealing contrast to the creamy richness of Gorgonzola dolce. With the more pungent Gorgonzola naturale, you will want a sweet wine, such as a Tuscan vin santo, a Malvasia delle Lipari, or a late-harvest Riesling. Fortified sweet wines, such as sherry and port, tend to accentuate the Gorgonzola's spiciness.*

GREAT HILL BLUE

Great Hill Dairy
Raw cow's milk
Massachusetts

A former dairy farmer, Tim Stone did not begin making cheese until he had sold his herd of cows. Commodity milk had not been a good business for him, but Stone began to think that cheesemaking might be. His informal market research suggested that there could be a niche for a mellow blue cheese made with raw, nonhomogenized milk.

Homogenization breaks down milk's fat globules so that they remain suspended, rather than rise to the top in a cream layer. Blue cheeses made with homogenized milk age faster, a boon to the bottom line, but they also tend to be more piquant, with an acidic finish and bite that Stone wanted to avoid.

Today, he buys his milk from several nearby farms in the Buzzards Bay area, 50 miles south of Boston. The six-pound wheels develop their blue veining from inoculation with *Penicillium roqueforti*, the same mold used to make Roquefort. The wheels mature for about six months in a thick plastic bag, which prevents a rind from forming. Like many other blues, Great Hill Blue is wrapped in foil before shipping to keep it from drying out.

This is a handsome cheese with a lot of personality. A wheel stands about three inches tall, with plentiful blue-gray veining in an off-white paste. The texture is creamy, especially at the heart, and the flavors are moderately piquant, with the lactic tang of buttermilk.

WINES THAT WORK: *Pour a botrytised dessert wine, such as Sauternes or Barsac, or a late-harvest Sauvignon Blanc from the New World.*

Cheese Platter Theme

Aging Gracefully

With the three goat cheeses on this platter, you can gain a sense of
the transformation that happens with time. The Green Peppercorn Cone (page 76)
has the moist interior typical of a cheese less than one month old.
Garrotxa (page 70), at six to eight weeks, has a firmer texture and more complexity.
Tumalo Tomme (page 132), aged the longest, has the most depth of flavor.
Age is only one of many elements that differentiate these cheeses,
but it's a key difference.

Garrotxa

Green Peppercorn Cone

Tumalo Tomme

< LEFT TO RIGHT: Green Peppercorn Cone, Garrotxa, Tumalo Tomme

GREEN PEPPERCORN CONE

 Coach Farm
Pasteurized goat's milk
New York

When Miles and Lillian Cahn bought an abandoned dairy farm two hours north of New York City in 1983, they imagined it as a weekend retreat from their busy weekdays running a handbag company, Coach Leatherware. They hoped to restore their new property as a working farm, making goat cheese for urban restaurants, but they did not envision themselves as full-time goat farmers. Within two years, however, they had sold their leather business to turn their attention and capital to their goats, now numbering about one thousand.

Coach Farm makes a range of goat cheeses, fresh and aged, but the Green Peppercorn Cone (pictured on pages 16, 74) is among the standouts. It is a truncated four-ounce pyramid with a bloomy rind and a soft interior perfumed with green peppercorns. (Coach Farm also makes the same cheese in a larger, brick shape.)

One hallmark of artisanal goat cheese, which Coach Farm's cheeses certainly are, is that the curds are carefully hand ladled, not mechanically pumped, into their molds. Goat curds are particularly delicate, so it is only through gentle handling that the cheesemaker can achieve the desired light texture in the finished cheese.

The bloomy rind develops gradually on the Green Peppercorn Cone during its three-week aging. These white surface molds ripen the cheese from the outside in, so you can expect the cheese to be creamier just under the rind than it is at the heart. You can identify a mature cheese by the state of the rind: it will begin to wrinkle and show some golden markings, a good clue that the interior is softening nicely. At perfect ripeness, the paste will be off-white, soft, and creamy, imbued with peppercorn flavor and finishing with a lemon-custard note.

WINES THAT WORK: *This delicate, creamy cheese calls for a light, crisp wine that will not overwhelm it. Sparkling wine, Sancerre, and dry rosé are three good choices.*

GRUYÈRE

(gree-YAIR)
Raw cow's milk
Switzerland

Gruyère production began hundreds of years ago in what is now the canton of Fribourg, in French-speaking western Switzerland. Today, the town of Gruyères—with an *s* on the end—is a tourist destination, a sign of the high regard cheese lovers around the world have for its namesake. Gruyère is a solid, dependable cheese in its youth, an exciting and memorable cheese when aged.

Most Gruyère is made with the combined milk of several farms, although some farmstead production persists. The evening milk is left to ripen overnight, which allows desirable bacteria to get a head start, and then pooled with the morning milk the next day. Once the curds form, they are cut small and heated in the whey, which lures out more whey and contributes to the tight, firm paste of the finished cheese. The fresh wheels are pressed and brined, and then they begin their long maturation.

Dairies typically keep the wheels for the first few weeks, giving them regular brine baths to seal the rind and turning them often to make sure the fat and moisture are evenly distributed. The wheels then go to an aging facility, where specialists monitor their care. At five months, they are deemed ready for release, but the better wheels will be kept for further aging, perhaps as long as twelve months.

Wheels that are at least a year old are entitled to the designation Réserve. Some producers mature them in natural caves and label them cave aged. Over time, these sixty-pound wheels darken internally, changing from ivory to gold, and the flavor and aromas intensify. Cave-aged Gruyère has pronounced brown-butter and nut aromas, with a pleasing balance of salt and sweet on the tongue. The texture is dense, firm, and smooth and the flavors long and concentrated.

WINES THAT WORK: *Match Gruyère's texture and intensity with a creamy white Burgundy or Chardonnay or an aromatic Pinot Gris. Dry or off-dry sherry will play off its nuttiness. Pinot Noir can also work, especially if the wine is more earthy than berrylike.*

HUDSON VALLEY CAMEMBERT

Old Chatham Sheepherding Company
Pasteurized cow's and sheep's milk
New York

Nancy and Tom Clark have the country's largest dairy sheep farm, in New York's Hudson Valley, and they make a variety of cheeses with their flock's ultrarich milk. For the Camembert, they mix the milk with cow's milk from their neighbor to achieve a blend of about 40 percent sheep's milk and 60 percent cow's milk. They also add some cream to make the finished cheese even richer, although not enough to put Hudson Valley Camembert in the category of a *triple crème* (page 143).

The dairy makes the cheese in three sizes: a four-ounce square, a one-pound round named Tom's Hudson Valley Camembert, and a two-pound round similarly named for Nancy. Go for the larger round if you can; it has the most appealing proportion of bloomy rind to creamy interior.

Although named for the well-known French cheese, Hudson Valley Camembert resembles Camembert hardly at all. It has a powdery white rind like its French namesake, from desirable surface molds that help the cheese ripen. But inside, Hudson Valley Camembert reveals its own unique character. The paste is ivory and supersoft, with a lush, buttery, tongue-coating texture and tart, nutty flavors that call to mind whipped crème fraîche. The rind is edible, but the cheese will be more compatible with wine if you cut it away.

Hudson Valley Camembert's richness is best appreciated at the end of a meal, with toasted walnut bread and pears or figs, perhaps, or a crisp green salad for balance.

WINES THAT WORK: *Contrast or complement? Sparkling wine makes a brisk palate cleanser for this unctuous, full-fat cheese. Alternatively, you can echo the cheese's buttery texture with a creamy malolactic Chardonnay from California or France.*

HUMBOLDT FOG

Cypress Grove Chevre
Pasteurized goat's milk
California

A unique soft-ripened goat cheese created in the early 1990s by Mary Keehn, Humboldt Fog (pictured on pages 8, 20, 126) has a thin line of gray ash in the middle. Standing out against the stark white of the paste, the ash ripple represents the coastal fog in Humboldt County, the rural region where the cheese is made.

Keehn buys her milk from local farms and makes several different goat cheeses with it, but Humboldt Fog is her flagship. Produced in two sizes, a fourteen-ounce and a five-pound wheel, the cheese ripens from the outside in, thanks to the work of the white molds on the rind. A wedge cut from a wheel—especially a large wheel—offers an appealing progression of textures, from creamy edge to firm center.

The milk for Humboldt Fog undergoes a slow overnight coagulation that allows flavor to build. The next day, the molds are half filled with the fresh curds, then sprinkled with a mixture of flavorless ash and salt and topped with the remaining curds. Once the wheels have drained and dried a bit, they are coated with more ash and sprayed with the mold spores that will eventually produce the soft, bloomy rind. The ash is not just aesthetic. It lowers the acidity on the surface of the cheese, making a more hospitable home for the molds. Ripening lasts three to four weeks.

Humboldt Fog has a straightforward, clean, and balanced flavor, with pleasing acidity and the salt level in check. It never has the strong goaty taste that mars some goat cheeses, a reflection of the quality of the milk.

WINES THAT WORK: *Enjoy Humboldt Fog with Sauvignon Blanc or Sancerre, with a dry rosé, or a medium-bodied Pinot Noir.*

IDIAZÁBAL

(ee-dee-ah-ZAH-bal)
Raw sheep's milk
Spain

The origins of this cheese reside in the tradition of the transhumance, the annual ritual of moving animals into the mountains to feed on spring and summer pasture, and then back down to valley shelters when cold weather threatens. In Spain's Basque region, shepherds made their spring and summer cheeses in mountain huts, bringing the wheels down to the market in the village of Idiazábal when they descended in the fall. The huts were heated with wood fires, so the cheeses gradually became infused with smoke, and the village customers came to like the taste. The smoked sheep's milk cheese from the mountains took the name of the town where it was sold.

Today, Ordizia has replaced Idiazábal as the market town, and it holds a festival every fall to celebrate the local smoked cheese. The cheesemakers compete for top honors in a juried tasting, and attendees pay a small fortune for a taste of the prizewinning wheel.

Unfortunately, artisanal Idiazábal is rare today. Most of it is made by a cooperative or in a factory, and quality consequently varies. The wheels typically weigh three to four pounds and are matured for at least two months, but more age improves them. The best Idiazábal will be firm but not dry, with a pronounced acidity and a rich, buttery sheep's milk taste subtly overlaid with smoke. Older wheels can be sharp, salty, and tangy and dry enough to grate. The cheese is easier to like before it reaches that stage.

WINES THAT WORK: *The smokiness of Idiazábal can be a challenge for wine. If the wheel is on the young side, it will go well with fino sherry; if it is drier, sharper, and more mature, look to a dry amontillado sherry or a robust red wine with restrained fruit, such as a young Rioja.*

LINCOLNSHIRE POACHER

Raw cow's milk
England

A farmstead cheese from Holstein milk, Lincolnshire Poacher debuted in 1992. Three years later, it won top honors at the British Cheese Awards, a remarkable feat for third-generation dairyman Simon Jones, a novice cheesemaker. But Jones had some accomplished mentors, including Jamie Montgomery of Montgomery's Cheddar, arguably England's finest Cheddar.

Jones and his wife, Janette, undertook cheesemaking when the price of commodity milk sunk low enough to endanger their dairy business. They follow many of the same steps used in Cheddar production (page 51): cutting the curds very small, cooking them until they are springy, gathering them in large blocks and stacking them repeatedly on one another, and then milling them until fine. Finally, the curds are salted, molded, and pressed for a couple of days. All these procedures help to expel whey and produce a firm cheese that benefits from long aging.

Wheels of Lincolnshire Poacher weigh about forty-five pounds and are matured for twelve to twenty months. During that time, they develop a hard natural rind and a dense interior the color of butterscotch. The cheese smells like butterscotch, too, or like the Mexican *dulce de leche*, with brown-butter notes, a caramel-like sweetness, and enough acidity and salt to keep the sweetness in check. The texture is creamier than that of most Cheddars, and the flavors last and last.

WINES THAT WORK: *The same wines that are pleasing with Cheddar can partner Lincolnshire Poacher. Pour a red wine with rich fruit, such as a Zinfandel or a Cabernet Sauvignon. An even better match is a nutty sherry—a dry or off-dry amontillado or oloroso—which has some of the same caramel notes.*

MAHÓN

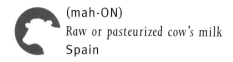

(mah-ON)
Raw or pasteurized cow's milk
Spain

The Spanish island of Minorca has a long history of dairy farming and cheesemaking, with the cheeses shipped abroad from the port of Mahón. The cheeses likely varied considerably in style in times past, but they were uniformly called *queso de Mahón* (cheese from Mahón). Today, Mahón is a DOP cheese (see page 142), so the process for making it is defined and regulated. Still, all Mahón is not alike.

Six hundred dairy farms on the island either make cheese or sell milk to others who do. The farmstead producers use raw milk and traditional methods, but a great deal of Mahón is now made industrially or in big cooperatives with pasteurized milk.

You can distinguish a farm-made cheese by the indentations from the cloth bag used to drain and shape the curds. Mahón is a thick, square cheese with rounded edges, traditionally formed by tying the four corners of the draining bag together and pressing to remove the whey. Large-scale dairies use plastic molds, so there are no surface markings.

As they age, the cheeses are rubbed with butter or olive oil to seal the rind, and sometimes with paprika to enhance the appearance. Maturation may vary from one month to one year, with aged cheeses showing far more character. Young Mahón is pale gold inside, semisoft and rather creamy, with a pronounced acidity and apparent salt. (It is said that even the cow's milk on Minorca is salty because of the sea breezes that spray the pastures.) The interior becomes golden and firmer as the cheese matures, and nut and caramel aromas develop that call to mind *dulce de leche*, the Mexican caramelized-milk dessert.

WINES THAT WORK: *With young Mahón, pour a young Spanish white wine, such as Albariño or Verdejo. The more mature cheese needs a wine with more intensity, preferably a red. Consider a Ribera del Duero or Syrah. An off-dry amontillado sherry is another good choice with aged Mahón.*

MAJORERO

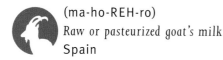

(ma-ho-REH-ro)
Raw or pasteurized goat's milk
Spain

Fuerteventura, the largest of Spain's Canary Islands, is the source of the delightful Majorero (pictured on page 110). The cheese's name derives from an old name for the island, Maxorata, meaning "the biggest one," a reference to the island's size. Enric Canut, a Spanish cheese authority, believes that Majorero is his country's finest goat cheese.

The goat breed used for Majorero yields particularly high-fat milk. You may even see droplets of fat on the cheese's cut surface. The islanders prefer their cheese fresh, at a week or two old, but most wheels for export are typically aged much longer than that and sometimes up to a year.

Artisanal production with raw milk persists on the island, but most Majorero is made in a big cooperative from pasteurized milk. The industrial product is a flat wheel weighing about seven pounds, with cross-hatching on the rind, while farmstead wheels vary more in size. Traditionally, cheeses intended for aging will be rubbed with olive oil, paprika, or roasted corn flour to slow moisture loss. Wheels destined for export don't usually get this protective treatment, however, as the rind must be clean and dry to withstand shipment in a vacuum package.

At two to three months of age, Majorero will have a smooth, semifirm, ivory interior, with perhaps a touch of chalkiness. The flavor will be tart, with a hint of lemon and possibly some nutty, cooked-milk smells.

WINES THAT WORK: *To accompany the cheese at the start of a meal, open a dry, fruity Spanish white, such as Verdejo or Albariño. At the end of a meal, pair Majorero with a nutty oloroso sherry for a lovely dessert.*

MANCHEGO

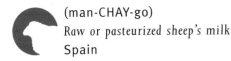

(man-CHAY-go)
Raw or pasteurized sheep's milk
Spain

Produced on the high plains of La Mancha in central Spain, Manchego (pictured on page 110) is without a doubt the country's most famous cheese. Cervantes described it in *Don Quixote* in 1605 ("harder than if it had been made of sand and lime," he wrote), but its origins are much earlier. La Mancha is a dry region of climatic extremes; the Arabs called it al-Ansha, "land without water."

Artisanal cheesemakers still use raw milk for Manchego, but far more cheese is made industrially, with pasteurized milk. Wheels receive a minimum of two months' aging, but often much more. Twelve- to fourteen-month-old Manchego is not uncommon at U.S. cheese counters, and it displays the concentrated flavor that comes with age.

In times past, Manchego was aged in esparto baskets, which left a zigzag impression on the rind. Today, cheesemakers rely on plastic molds to produce the pattern, which some other Manchego-style cheeses have as well.

Manchego is drum-shaped and weighs four to eight pounds. Young wheels sometimes have an aroma of sour cream or cheesecake. As they age, the fragrance becomes nuttier and the tangy flavor more mellow, full, and lingering. The interior is firm and dry, ivory to butter colored, with the glistening surface typical of cheeses made from high-fat sheep's milk.

Every tapas bar in Spain serves Manchego, traditionally cut into thin triangles and sometimes accompanied by quince paste, a sweet contrast to the cheese's salty bite.

WINES THAT WORK: *Serve Manchego before dinner with a fino or manzanilla sherry to echo the cheese's sharp saltiness. At the end of the meal, a big red wine, such as a Rioja or Ribera del Duero from Spain or a Corbières or Coteaux du Languedoc from southwest France, is more appealing.*

MIMOLETTE

(mee-mo-LET)
Pasteurized cow's milk
France

With its strident pumpkin orange color and moonscapelike rind, Mimolette draws attention at the cheese counter. Made in far northern France and at several dairies in Normandy, it resembles Dutch Edam, said to be its inspiration. According to legend, the French devised Mimolette in the seventeenth century when a ban on imports made their beloved Dutch cheese unavailable.

Resembling a bowling ball flattened at both poles, Mimolette varies in size from five to nine pounds. Some also know it as Boule (ball) de Lille, a reference to its peculiar shape and to the city in northern France where the wheels were reportedly aged in the past. By either name, it owes its head-turning color to annatto, a plant-based natural dye.

Matured anywhere from three to twenty-four months, Mimolette becomes drier, saltier, more piquant, and more brittle and waxy as it ages. In youth, it is semihard and mild; as time passes, the paste deepens to the color of dried mango, a butterscotch aroma develops, and the taste intensifies. Age also produces a thick, rough, pockmarked rind.

WINES THAT WORK: *With a young Mimolette, consider a dry fino sherry. More mature wheels need wine with more intensity and weight, such as an Alsatian Pinot Gris (Tokay d'Alsace), Austrian Grüner Veltliner on the rich end of its spectrum, or a full-bodied, buttery California Chardonnay. A dry or off-dry amontillado sherry resonates with the cheese's caramel notes.*

MONTASIO

(mohn-TAHZ-yo)
Pasteurized cow's milk
Italy

A mountain cheese made for centuries in the northeastern corner of Italy, near the Austrian border, Montasio can withstand long aging. Some wheels are matured for a year or more and become hard enough to grate finely, like Parmigiano-Reggiano. Aged five to ten months, the cheese is known as *mezzano*, or semiaged, and is a delightful and well-priced table cheese. Even younger wheels—the cheese is aged for a minimum of two months—have considerable flavor, but they develop more aroma and concentration as they mature. The date of production is stamped on the rind, so a merchant should be able to tell you the age of the cheese you are purchasing, although color, aroma, and texture are good clues.

Montasio's thin, natural rind becomes harder and darker as the cheese matures. The internal color also deepens, from ivory to gold. A wheel of medium maturity will have a compact, semifirm texture and a paste the color of butter. The aroma may remind you of warm butter or crème fraîche, with an animal scent in the background. Let a nugget dissolve on your tongue and you will notice the pronounced acidity, a sour-cream tang balanced with a sweet finish.

To make a cheese, like Montasio, with potential to age, the cheesemaker must drive moisture from the curds. Many steps assist in the process: cutting the just-formed curd very small, the size of rice grains in the case of Montasio; heating the cut curds to tighten them and draw out more whey; and pressing the day-old wheels to eliminate yet more moisture. A low-moisture, salty cheese like Montasio does not support the growth of spoilage bacteria, so the wheels can age safely at length.

WINES THAT WORK: *Many different wines are pleasing with Montasio, despite the cheese's prominent acidity. Among whites, consider a dry Riesling, a creamy Chardonnay (but without obvious oak), a Viognier, or a Greco di Tufo. Choose a red wine of some intensity, such as Barbera, Barolo, or Barbaresco from Piedmont; Merlot; Syrah; or Cabernet Sauvignon.*

MONTE ENEBRO

(MOHN-tay ay-NAY-bro)
Pasteurized goat's milk
Spain

In 1982, at the age of sixty-four, Rafael Báez launched his goat dairy with this unusual and distinctive cheese. Báez had studied cheesemaking with Enric Canut, a renowned Spanish advocate of traditional practices, and Monte Enebro (pictured on page 15) is the successful product of this apprenticeship.

Báez buys his milk and makes his cheese in the Valle del Tiétar, thirty miles southwest of Madrid. A long, flattened log weighing about two pounds, Monte Enebro is a beautiful sight on a cheese tray. Its dimpled rind resembles the bark of a birch tree thanks to the thick dusting of blue-gray and white molds that develop over the cheese's three-week maturation. Inside, the paste is chalk white to off-white, a reminder that goat's milk, unlike cow's milk, has no carotene.

The surface molds ripen the cheese from the outside in, so the paste will be creamier just under the rind and firmer toward the core. On the tongue, the cheese is dense and silky, with a buttery, melt-in-your-mouth quality. The scent is herbaceous and piney. Monte Enebro does not lack for salt, and it can be pungent when mature, especially near the rind. You will need to cut the rind away if you hope to find a complementary wine.

WINES THAT WORK: *Avoid sweet or even off-dry whites and tannic reds, but virtually any other wine will suit this cheese. Grüner Veltliner, Sauvignon Blanc, dry rosé, Pinot Noir, and Beaujolais are all good companions.*

French Classics

Coming from all corners of France, the cheeses on this platter are all exemplars of their type: the nutty alpine cheese Abondance (page 26); the pungent, washed-rind Munster-Géromé (page 98); the iconic Basque sheep's milk cheese, Ossau-Iraty (page 101); Roquefort (page 121), the country's most esteemed blue; and the pyramidal Valençay (page 135), emblematic of the Loire Valley's delicate goat cheeses. (See page 141 for a list of French cheeses included in this book.)

Abondance

Munster-Géromé

Ossau-Iraty

Roquefort

Valençay

< CLOCKWISE FROM TOP: *Ossau-Iraty, Abondance, Valençay, Munster-Géromé, Roquefort*

MORBIER

(MOR-bee-yay)
Raw cow's milk
France

Made in the mountainous region of the Franche-Comté, in eastern France, Morbier owes its existence to bad weather. In times past, when winter turned harsh in the mountains, the isolated farmers could not get their milk to the village dairy, so they devised a smaller cheese they could make on the farm.

Traditionally, Morbier uses the milk from both morning and evening milkings, which explains the ash layer in the middle. The farmer would curdle the evening milk over a wood fire, then transfer the curds to molds and sprinkle ash over them to keep them from forming a skin. The next day, the morning milk would be transformed into curds and spread over the ash. The wheel would then be pressed, salted, and matured for about forty-five days, during which its exterior would be frequently washed with brine.

Most Morbier is no longer made on farms but in large cooperative dairies or factories. The dividing layer is vegetable ash now, not wood ash, and the practice of separating evening and morning curds is probably only observed on some farms.

Morbier is a round, flat cheese, two to three inches in height and weighing anywhere from seven to seventeen pounds. It has an orange-tinged, salty, slightly crunchy rind as a result of the repeated washings. The interior is semifirm, dense, and creamy, with a few small eyes and the thin line of gray ash slashing the middle. The aroma is mild and faintly meaty, the flavor a little sweet, but most Morbier does not have a pronounced character. If you are lucky, you may find one that has been given extended cellar time by an *affineur* (cheese ager), such as the renowned Jean d'Alos. With three to four months of watchful aging, Morbier becomes another cheese entirely, with seductive aromas of mushroom and earth.

WINES THAT WORK: *Sparkling wine provides textural contrast to Morbier's dense creaminess; a Pinot Gris with some viscosity will echo the texture. Both approaches work. Dry amontillado sherry, another appropriate option, complements the cheese's nutty notes.*

MOZZARELLA DI BUFALA

(mohtz-ah-RELL-ah dee BOO-fah-lah)
Pasteurized water buffalo's milk
Italy

Resembling the bison that once roamed the American West, water buffalo now thrive in the marshes around Naples. Although Mozzarella from their milk has been made at least since the late 1700s, the animals suffered during World War II and were nearly exterminated by the retreating Nazis. But they have been reintroduced successfully, and production of Mozzarella di Bufala thrives, to the delight of the many who find it superior to cow's milk Mozzarella.

Unlike cow's milk, buffalo's milk has no carotene, so the cheese it yields is whiter. It also has almost twice the fat of cow's milk, which produces a creamier cheese, and its flavor is more pronounced, a little gamier.

To make Mozzarella di Bufala, the fresh milk is cultured with whey from the previous day's production and coagulated with rennet. After the curds form, they are allowed to ripen for several hours in their whey, then they are transferred to boiling water and heated until they are stretchable. Workers reach into the hot water and deftly mold the malleable curd into balls. The sooner it is eaten after that, the better. The residents around Naples pride themselves on their access to still-warm Mozzarella and say that by the time it gets to Rome, it is too old.

Try to buy Mozzarella di Bufala from a store that gets air shipments often and sells the cheese quickly. The ball should have a thin, tight skin and the interior should be firm and compact yet creamy, with a sweet, milky taste. You should be able to make a neat slice that holds together, perfect for layering with tomatoes and basil.

WINES THAT WORK: *Mozzarella di Bufala is an antipasto cheese, so you will want a light, zippy, appetite-arousing wine, such as Fiano di Avellino, Vermentino, Pinot Grigio, or a dry rosé.*

MUNSTER-GÉROMÉ

(MUN-ster zhay-row-MAY)
Raw (rare) and pasteurized cow's milk
France

More commonly known as Munster, even in France, the famous Alsatian washed-rind cheese is officially Munster-Géromé. That appellation covers both the Munster made on the eastern side of the Vosges Mountains in Alsace and the nearly identical cheese, Géromé, made on the western slope, in Lorraine. Let's call it Munster for short.

With a history that goes back to the seventh century, Munster is one of France's oldest cheeses, attributed to a Benedictine monastery. The monks perfected the art of curing cheeses by repeatedly rubbing them with a brine-soaked cloth, a practice that created a moist, salty rind that encouraged some bacteria and discouraged less desirable yeasts and molds. The orange coloration that develops on a Munster rind over time is a sign that the good bacteria are on the job, contributing to the transformation of the cheese's aroma, texture, and flavor.

To produce a semisoft cheese like Munster, the fresh curds are cut large to retain moisture. They are packed into molds and allowed to drain naturally, without pressing. The wheels are considered ready in three weeks or so, depending on their size, but flavor improves and aroma heightens over the next couple of months. The cheese is made in a range of sizes, from le petit Munster weighing four to eight ounces to larger wheels of about two pounds.

A ripe Munster has a reddish orange rind, an appetizing barnyard fragrance, a supple, slightly sticky texture, and a robust flavor. Don't trim away the rind. Its salty crunch provides a contrast to the creamy interior. In Alsace, people enjoy Munster with a few caraway seeds or with boiled potatoes in their skins.

WINES THAT WORK: *Such a fragrant and palate-coating cheese needs an equally aromatic white wine with viscosity. The best choice is a Gewürztraminer, Pinot Gris (Tokay d'Alsace), or Riesling from Alsace.*

ORIGINAL BLUE

Point Reyes Farmstead Cheese Company
Raw cow's milk
California

Bob Giacomini knew that his four daughters didn't want to run his Marin County dairy farm when he retired. But nobody wanted to sell the family property, either, with its rolling hills and Tomales Bay view. The challenge: to find a value-added use for the farm's milk that would engage and support the next generation. The solution: Original Blue, an aged cheese from the family's own herd and the only blue made in California.

The Giacominis hired Monte McIntyre, who had long made the popular Maytag blue, as their cheesemaker. The first wheels debuted in 2000 and quickly found an audience. The morning milk goes straight from the milking parlor to the cheesemaking vat, where it is cultured, coagulated with rennet, and inoculated with *Penicillium roqueforti*. The fresh curds are drained in hoops until they are firm enough to unmold, then the chalk white wheels are salted all over and pierced to admit air. The wheels spend three to four weeks in unsealed bags in a curing room, waiting for the blue veins to emerge.

When the blue has advanced sufficiently, the bags are sealed and the wheels are transferred to cold storage, where they will spend about six months, becoming creamier and fuller in flavor with the passage of time. As customers order them, the rindless wheels will be cleaned up, wrapped in foil, and shipped.

A wheel of Original Blue weighs about six and a half pounds and measures about eight inches in diameter. With its blue-gray veins snaking through the pale paste, the cheese looks like a chunk of fine marble. On the tongue, it is moist, dense, and creamy, with a robust buttermilk tang.

WINES THAT WORK: *That cultured-milk flavor in Original Blue is hard on wine. Best bets are medium- to full-bodied whites with restrained oak and alcohol. Grüner Veltliner from Austria and Pinot Gris from Alsace and Oregon typically have enough body and acidity to complement this creamy cheese.*

OSSAU-IRATY

(OH-so ear-ah-TEE)
Raw or pasteurized sheep's milk
France

Sheep's milk cheeses have been made in the Basque region of the Pyrenees for hundreds of years and have probably not changed much over the centuries. Shepherds still take their flocks into the mountains in spring to take advantage of the lush pasture, gradually working their way up and then back down again as cold weather threatens. But not until 1980 did these skilled artisans receive AOC certification (see page 142) for their cheese, an appellation that joins two place-names, the Ossau Valley and the Iraty Forest, to designate the traditional cheese of the region.

About sixty producers still make Ossau-Iraty (pictured on page 92) on the farm; the rest is made in larger dairies with pooled milk. If you travel in the region, you will see roadside signs advertising cheese for sale at the local farmhouses. Don't pass it up.

Wheels, which range from about four to fifteen pounds, are lightly pressed and periodically rubbed with brine to develop the rind. They are matured for two to six months, becoming drier, nuttier, and spicier as they age. At two months, the interior will be semifirm, smooth, and mild; at six months, it is firm and a little granular. Sheep's milk is particularly high in fat, a fact evidenced by the droplets of fat that sometimes emerge on the cut surface of the cheese at room temperature.

Abbaye de Belloc is a superb raw-milk Ossau-Iraty worth looking for. Once produced at the abbey by Benedictine monks, it is now made in a nearby dairy according to the monks' recipe. It has lovely aromas of brown butter and caramel.

In restaurants in the Basque region, Ossau-Iraty is often presented with a jar of cherry preserves. The contrast of sweet jam and salty cheese is delightful.

WINES THAT WORK: *Ossau-Iraty is a wine-friendly cheese. At the start of a meal, serve it with fino sherry to complement its nuttiness, or with Pinot Gris or Bordeaux Blanc, a textural match. At the end of a meal, try a medium-weight red, such as Merlot, or an off-dry amontillado sherry. The robust red wines from southwest France, such as Irouléguy and Madiran, will work if the cheese is more mature.*

PARMIGIANO-REGGIANO

(par-mi-JAH-no reh-JAH-no)
Raw cow's milk
Italy

Many Americans use Parmigiano-Reggiano only as a grating cheese, but it belongs on the cheese board, too. Some connoisseurs consider it the finest cheese in the world, bar none. It is certainly one of the most imitated, but the imitations never come close to the original's complexity.

More than five hundred dairies in five provinces around Parma and Bologna make Parmigiano-Reggiano, following the strict procedures laid out by the producer consortium. Evening milk is allowed to stand overnight, then skimmed the next day. The whole morning milk is added, and the mix is cultured with whey from the previous day's cheesemaking, which seeds the milk with the bacteria responsible for the cheese's ultimate flavor.

The young wheels of Parmigiano-Reggiano spend three weeks or more in a brine to season the cheese and establish the hard rind. Then comes the long aging phase— a minimum of twelve months, but often two to three years—that produces the cheese's crumbly yet creamy texture and inimitable fragrance.

Weighing in at about eighty-five pounds, a wheel of Parmigiano-Reggiano will have an ivory paste in its youth, with aromas of milk and fresh grass. As it matures, the color deepens to straw, gold, and eventually amber, and more nutty, toasty, and brown-butter aromas develop. Experts often note both a hint of orange peel and a savory meat-broth aroma in mature Parmigiano-Reggiano. The crunchy nuggets that develop in older wheels are amino acid crystals, a sign that the cheese is well matured.

At the table, provide a blunt cheese knife that will break the Parmigiano into chunks. Slicing the cheese would compromise its texture.

WINES THAT WORK: *Serve chunks of Parmigiano-Reggiano before dinner with sparkling wine or Tocai Friulano. At the end of the meal, accompany the cheese with a medium- to full-bodied red that will match its intensity, such as Barbaresco or another Nebbiolo-based red, Merlot, Cabernet Sauvignon, or Zinfandel. A dry amontillado sherry is another fine match.*

PECORINO TOSCANO

(peh-coh-REE-noh toh-SCAH-noh)
Raw or pasteurized sheep's milk
Italy

One of Italy's most ancient cheeses, Pecorino Toscano has at least a two-thousand-year history. We can't know whether the Tuscan pecorino Pliny wrote about resembled today's cheeses, but the practice of turning sheep's milk into cheese remains widespread in the area. In fact, the designated zone for Pecorino Toscano DOP (see page 142) extends beyond Tuscany to include parts of neighboring regions.

Hundreds of producers make Pecorino Toscano, and because the procedures are not rigorously regimented, the resulting cheeses are not identical. Some cheesemakers rub their wheels with tomato paste to color the rind and enhance the flavor. A few make the cheese with raw milk. But the most obvious difference is in the age of the wheels, which can vary from twenty days to six months or more.

To make a fresh Pecorino Toscano, the cheesemaker cuts the curd into relatively large nuggets, the size of hazelnuts. For a Pecorino Toscano *stagionato*, a cheese designed for aging, the curd is cut smaller, to release more whey. Wheels intended for aging are pressed to firm them, then brined or dry-salted. As they ripen, they are massaged with olive oil to discourage mold. They must spend at least four months in the aging cellar, while fresh cheeses can be on the market in about three weeks.

Fresh Pecorino Toscano is mild and moist, with the sweet, uncomplicated flavor of fresh milk. The aged wheels develop a thin, golden rind and a firm, smooth, butter-colored interior. Despite their age, they retain a milky sweetness, with nut and caramel notes developing as the cheese matures.

WINES THAT WORK: *Choose your wine according to the age of the cheese. Fresh Pecorino Toscano wants a crisp white, such as Pinot Grigio or Fiano di Avellino. For a more mature cheese with nutty notes, look for a Tuscan red, such as Chianti Classico, or a California Sangiovese.*

PIAVE

(pee-AH-vay)
Pasteurized cow's milk
Italy

Made by a cooperative dairy in the province of Belluno, in Italy's Veneto region, Piave debuted in 1960, and is now the dairy's best-selling cheese. It is named for a local river and patterned after a traditional cheese of the area.

In the late 1800s, when many rural people were leaving Belluno in search of work and small cheesemakers were struggling to survive, a local priest suggested establishing a cooperative. Initially, his idea was for individual cheesemakers to share a single production facility, with each making his or her cheeses in turn. This was a novel approach at the time, and it gave many cheesemakers an alternative to emigration. Gradually, the concept evolved into the type of dairy cooperative we know today, where farmers pool their milk and make cheese jointly.

Piave is sold at three stages: *fresco*, or fresh, twenty to sixty days old; *mezzano*, or semiaged, two to six months old; and *vecchio*, or aged, more than six months old. Not surprisingly, the *vecchio* has the most compelling flavor, an interplay of sweet and salty that makes you crave another taste. As it matures beyond six months, it develops the toasted-nut aroma of Gruyère, the dense texture of a young Parmigiano-Reggiano, and the sweet-salt balance of an aged Gouda. Irresistible.

A wheel weighs about fifteen pounds but is only about two inches tall, so it is a cheese of imposing diameter. The rind is repeatedly impressed with the name, while inside, the pale gold, dense, and firm paste has a caramel fragrance and enough acidity to balance the sweetness.

WINES THAT WORK: *Piave's sweet, concentrated flavor works best with richer white wines, such as Chardonnay (preferably without obvious oak), and with medium-weight reds, such as Merlot and some Zinfandels. Also consider a Madeira or off-dry amontillado sherry to complement the cheese's sweetness.*

PLEASANT RIDGE RESERVE

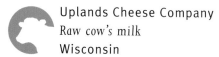

Uplands Cheese Company
Raw cow's milk
Wisconsin

The two couples who own Uplands Cheese Company began dairy farming together in the mid-1990s for economy of scale. They soon realized that the milk from their pasture-raised animals was of exceptional quality, too good to sell as commodity milk. After some research, they settled on the idea of making a long-aged, raw-milk cheese in the style of France's alpine specialties, Beaufort (page 33) and Comté (page 52), albeit smaller. The ten-pound Pleasant Ridge Reserve (pictured on pages 7, 126) is the award-winning outcome.

Rare among American cheeses, Pleasant Ridge Reserve is made with the unpasteurized milk of a single herd and only during pasture season—in Wisconsin, from late spring until fall. The owners believe that the lush fresh grasses and wildflowers that comprise the cows' diet during that time enhance the milk, producing desirable flavors that are absent when the cows are on hay.

Wheels of Pleasant Ridge Reserve are repeatedly rubbed by hand with brine and turned during their minimum four-month aging. The brine keeps undesirable molds at bay while allowing flavor- and aroma-imparting bacteria to do their work.

Pleasant Ridge Reserve has a thin, hard natural rind and a firm, smooth, yellow-gold interior. Four-month-old wheels are moister than Beaufort or Comté, but more mature wheels—the ones you are likely to find in late winter and early spring—have a drier texture and more intensity. Even in youth, the cheese smells wonderfully of roasted peanuts and bacon, with a hint of caramel. The flavor is mellow, nutty, and moderately salty.

WINES THAT WORK: *Its well-integrated, balanced flavors make Pleasant Ridge Reserve easy on most wines. Partner it with a dry Pinot Gris or Riesling, a French Chablis, or an unoaked New World Chardonnay. If you prefer a red, look to a medium-weight wine, such as Pinot Noir. More mature wheels can take a more robust wine.*

PONT-L'ÉVÊQUE

(pohn leh VECK)
Raw or pasteurized cow's milk
France

One of France's oldest cheeses, Pont-l'Évêque traces its roots to the twelfth century and is thought to be the creation of Cistercian monks. Although most of the production is industrial now, using pasteurized milk, a little raw-milk farmstead Pont-l'Évêque still exists and would be worth seeking out in the best cheese shops in Paris and Normandy. Such a product would be illegal for sale in the United States because it is a soft cheese aged less than sixty days.

Pont-l'Évêque is made only in Normandy and in Mayenne, one of the *départements* of the Loire. The regulations permit several sizes, but the cheese is always square. A typical Pont-l'Évêque weighs about twelve ounces and is about four inches square and a little over an inch thick. The rind should have plentiful golden orange coloration, signaling the presence of flavor-producing bacteria. These bacteria, which emerge on the white surface of the young cheese over the six weeks or so that it ages, help to soften the interior and produce the dirty-socks aroma characteristic of washed-rind cheeses.

The cheese is not as strong as it smells. Inside, the butter-colored paste should be soft and supple, not runny, with a few small eyes. The flavor will be moderately salty and highly savory, with agreeable mushroom notes. Taste before you buy and avoid Pont-l'Évêque with a bitter finish. If you purchase and serve a whole square, the proper way to cut it is in triangles from the midpoint.

WINES THAT WORK: *A velvety Chardonnay or white Burgundy makes a pleasing textural and aromatic partner for this cheese as long as the wine doesn't have a lot of alcohol, oak, or sprightly fruit flavors. For a red wine, consider a medium-weight Pinot Noir, which would match the cheese in intensity and complement its mushroom aroma.*

Salute to Spain

This collection highlights just a handful of the outstanding cheeses from Spain (see page 141), many of them little known in the United States until the recent past. Joining Manchego (page 87), the familiar but always enjoyable sheep's milk cheese, is a lesser-known goat cheese—Majorero (page 86) from the Canary Islands— and the pungent leaf-wrapped blue from the far north, Valdeón (page 134).

Majorero

Manchego

Valdeón

< CLOCKWISE FROM TOP RIGHT: *Valdeón, Manchego, Majorero*

QUESO DE LA SERENA

(KAY-so deh lah seh-RAY-nah)
Raw sheep's milk
Spain

The prized Merino sheep has long been the mainstay of animal husbandry in Spain's poor Extremadura region, where there are more sheep than people. For centuries, the shepherds of La Serena—literally, "the calm place"—in southeastern Extremadura, have raised their flocks for meat and wool, making a little cheese two to three months each year for their own and local consumption. But in the late 1980s, the price of wool plummeted, and the shepherds began counting on cheese for more revenue. Aficionados embraced their exquisite cheese and production has climbed, although it remains artisanal.

The Merino breed produces high-quality milk but not much of it. A farmer needs ten sheep to produce enough milk for a pound of cheese. It is hardly surprising, then, that Queso de la Serena is one of the most expensive cheeses in Spain.

Rare among cheeses, Queso de la Serena is coagulated with an enzyme extracted from a plant, the bitter *Cynara cardunculus*, an artichoke relative. The coagulation happens very slowly, allowing the curds to develop a lot of flavor and acidity. The enzyme also comes into play later, as the cheese matures. It breaks down the milk proteins, producing an exceptionally creamy—even runny—cheese over time. The classic way to eat a ripe Queso de la Serena is to cut off the top and dig in with a spoon.

Wheels range from about one and a half to four and a half pounds. They are briefly brined or dry salted early in the production process, then aged for a minimum of two months. At two months, the cheese has an unctuous, oozy texture, an appetizing cultured-milk aroma, and a pronounced lactic tang. You may perceive a slight bitter note, a legacy of the plant enzyme. Chances are, you will not find a wheel that is ripe enough to be spoonable, so cut it into wedges and enjoy the crunch of the salty rind against the creamy interior.

WINES THAT WORK: *A young Rioja or other Tempranillo-based red wine has enough personality for this highly flavored cheese and enough acidity and tannin to cleanse the palate.*

RACLETTE

(rah-KLETT)
Raw or pasteurized cow's milk
France and Switzerland

The Swiss claim *raclette* as practically their national dish, reveling in the simple peasant meal of melted cheese, boiled potatoes, pickled cocktail onions, and cornichons. It is traditionally made with a wheel of cow's milk cheese from the mountains of western Switzerland. The wheel is cut in half vertically and the cut side is held over a wood fire until the surface becomes molten. Then, with a knife, the *raclette* cook scrapes the warm, gooey melted cheese onto waiting plates, and diners enjoy it quickly, before it cools, coming back for more helpings as long as appetite allows.

On both the French and the Swiss side of the Alps, producers make a cheese they call Raclette, intended for this rib-sticking fireplace meal. The French version is usually raw milk; the Swiss cheese is typically from pasteurized milk. Other than that, the cheeses are similar. They weigh ten to fifteen pounds and have a butter-colored, semi-soft interior that is smooth and creamy, even a little sticky, with that roasted-peanut or meat-locker aroma that distinguishes many washed-rind cheeses. The natural rind is tinged with gold or orange and often tacky to the touch. Aficionados always want to get a bit of the softened, salt-crusted rind in their *raclette* portion.

Well-equipped cookware stores sell electric devices for preparing *raclette* at home, but it is arguably more enjoyable in a restaurant, when someone else does the work of monitoring and scraping the cheese. (Raclette comes from the French verb *racler*, meaning "to scrape.") Classically, it is made in a fireplace and enjoyed after a hard day on the ski slopes, but in truth it is hard to resist at any time of year. And the cheese is perfectly enjoyable on a cheese board, with no melting required.

WINES THAT WORK: *An aromatic dry Riesling with some body and spice matches Raclette's big flavors.*

REBLOCHON DE SAVOIE

(Ruh-blow-SHAWN duh sah-VWAH)
Raw cow's milk
France

Sadly, authentic Reblochon (pictured on page 11) is no longer available in the United States due to tightened Food and Drug Administration (FDA) regulations. Because it is made with raw milk and the FDA considers it a soft cheese—although the French don't—it is illegal for sale here. At least one producer has responded by creating a Reblochon-like cheese expressly for the United States, with lower moisture content and longer aging. Called Fromage de Savoie, it resembles Reblochon but does not rival it in texture or flavor.

We must go to France, then, to experience true Reblochon, a cheese made for centuries in the picturesque Savoy region. Its name comes from the verb *reblocher*, "to milk a cow again." According to legend, the Savoy cowherds of long ago leased their pasture from wealthy landowners and paid in proportion to the amount of milk they produced. Once a year, the landlord showed up to measure the cows' daily output and figure the annual rent. On that day, the cows' owner would not extract all the milk from the udders, so his yield looked low. Only when the landlord left would he finish the milking, using that "off-the-books" milk, which was richer than the initial milking, for his own cheese.

Today, Reblochon is still made on the farm, as well as in larger dairies. Farm cheeses bear a green stamp; cooperative or factory cheeses have a red stamp. On the farm, the cheese is made twice daily, after each milking, and there are no days off.

A ripe Reblochon weighs a little over one pound and has a smooth, golden to orange rind with a dusting of white mold. The moist, supple interior is ivory and semisoft, with a few small eyes. Expect plentiful aromas of mushrooms, earth, and garlic.

WINES THAT WORK: *Among the best wines for Reblochon are the aromatic dry whites from Alsace, such as Pinot Gris (Tokay d'Alsace) and Pinot Blanc. A medium- to full-bodied Pinot Noir or red Burgundy with moderate alcohol can also be successful.*

RED HAWK

Cowgirl Creamery
Pasteurized cow's milk
California

Organic milk from a neighboring dairy provides the raw material for this washed-rind cheese from western Marin County. Its *triple-crème* designation (see page 143) indicates that the milk was enriched with cream to elevate the fat content, and the lusciousness quotient, in the finished cheese.

Red Hawk is a small disk, weighing about twelve ounces and measuring less than two inches high. The reddish orange mottling on the surface signals the presence of desirable bacteria that will ripen the cheese from the outside in and contribute mightily to its flavor. The cheese is rubbed with brine three times during its six-week maturation, not only to season it, but also to create the moist, salty surface that the "good" bacteria like. Some cheesemakers must inoculate the milk with these bacteria to get them to grow, but they are present naturally in the moist, humid air at Cowgirl Creamery, a stone's throw from the Pacific Ocean.

Although the cheese leaves the dairy at six weeks, it needs another couple of weeks to reach full maturity. A ripe Red Hawk will give to gentle pressure, and the reddish orange bacteria will be abundant on the surface. Inside, the cheese will be the color of butter, with a moist, semisoft, rich, spreadable texture and potent aromas of yeast, mushroom, and earth. The thin rind is edible and offers a faint salty crunch.

To appreciate this cheese at its best, take it out of its wrapper a day ahead so the rind can dry. Keep it at room temperature, covered with a cheese dome or inverted bowl, until you are ready to serve it.

WINES THAT WORK: *This pungent cheese is a difficult match for wine. Sparkling wine stands up to it, and the bubbles help rinse the palate, while a rich, spicy Gewürztraminer has the necessary intensity. Red wines are less promising.*

ROGUE RIVER BLUE

Rogue Creamery
Raw cow's milk
Oregon

David Gremmels and Cary Bryant had no cheesemaking experience when they purchased the seventy-year-old Rogue Creamery in 2002. But the creamery's former owner, Ig Vella (page 56), took the young men under his wing, mentoring and monitoring them during the transition. Vella's father had started the creamery, and Vella was eager to keep the business in the hands of owner-operators, even if he had to teach them cheesemaking himself. Together, the new owners have revived the Central Point, Oregon, dairy, which had fallen on hard times.

Gremmels and Bryant make several blue cheeses, but Rogue River Blue (pictured on page 58) is their most acclaimed and most scarce. They make it only with autumn milk from their neighbor's pasture-fed animals, convinced that this late-season milk is superior. The five-pound wheels age for a minimum of eight months, and at about the halfway point, they are enrobed in grape leaves that have steeped for months in Oregon pear brandy.

The long, slow aging produces a particularly creamy and buttery blue cheese with a vigorous but balanced flavor. It lacks the aggressive bite and saltiness that make some blue cheeses hard to love. Even people who shy away from blue cheeses will find Rogue River Blue approachable. Like many blue cheeses, it may "weep" as it comes to room temperature. To avoid trapping the moisture, be sure to unwrap it before allowing it to warm up, and pat it dry with a paper towel if needed.

WINES THAT WORK: *This elegant cheese needs a refined dessert wine, such as a Sauternes or botrytised Sauvignon Blanc, or a fortified wine such as Madeira or port.*

RONCAL

(rohn-KAHL)
Raw sheep's milk
Spain

Since the Middle Ages, the villages in Spain's Roncal Valley have managed the area's pasture jointly, an early example of enlightened environmentalism. To avoid overgrazing, the valley's management determines when the sheep will move into the high summer pastures, and when the flocks will descend in the fall. Prime pastureland is divided equitably, instilling a sense of community and shared resources. This model system has helped preserve the culture and ecology of the region.

Legend has it that the aged cheese from Roncal sustained the hordes of religious pilgrims en route to Santiago de Compostela in the Middle Ages. Then as now, the cheese was built to last.

Roncal is made only between December and July, when the sheep are on pasture. In late summer, the ewes are impregnated and cheesemaking ceases. Wheels typically weigh five to seven pounds and stand four to five inches high. To guarantee the cheese's longevity, the fresh wheels are pressed to expel excess moisture, then steeped in brine for about thirty-six hours. This lengthy salt bath establishes the rind, which will harden further during a minimum of four months in the aging cellar.

A firm-textured, somewhat crumbly cheese, Roncal has an herbaceous perfume with the wet-wool and animal aromas that turn up in many aged sheep's milk cheeses. The flavor is piquant but not sharp, with a full complement of salt and acidity but not too much of either. Underappreciated in the United States, it is an expertly made and beautifully balanced cheese with a long aftertaste.

WINES THAT WORK: *If you are serving Roncal before dinner, perhaps as a tapa with green olives, pour a fino or manzanilla sherry. At the end of a meal, turn to a full-bodied Spanish red, such as a Monastrell-based wine from Jumilla or a Ribera del Duero.*

ROQUEFORT

(roke-FORE)
Raw sheep's milk
France

France's most famous blue cheese requires the milk of more than two thousand farms and the labor of almost five thousand people. Yet there are only eight firms that actually make the cheese, ranging from very small (Carles) to large (Société). Although the milk may come from a wide swath of south-central France, the cheese must spend time ripening in caves under the village of Roquefort to earn the name.

As the fresh curds are packed into their molds, they are sprinkled with a powder that will produce the blue veins in the weeks ahead. In a process unique to Roquefort, this inoculant is made from rye bread that has been seeded with a selected strain of spores. The mold grows up in the bread, which is then dried and powdered. Roquefort producers bake rye bread once a year to create their annual supply of inoculant.

After about ten days at the dairy, while the six-pound wheels are still white, they are transferred to the Combalou caves and pierced to introduce air. Over the three weeks or so that the wheels spend in the cave, the blue veins will develop, stopping short of the salty edges. They then spend a minimum of another three months in cold storage before release, gradually developing piquancy and a creamy texture.

A well-made Roquefort will have evenly distributed veins in a moist, ivory paste. The cheese should be smooth, not granular, and it should hold together when sliced. Above all, look for balanced flavors. Roquefort is always bold and spicy, but it should not be harsh, bitter, or excessively salty. Some people like to cut Roquefort's strength with butter, although purists disdain the practice. Experts say the cheese is at its best in fall and winter because the wheels were made with the flavorful milk of grass-fed animals.

WINES THAT WORK: *Roquefort's spice and salt call for a rich dessert wine, such as Sauternes, Banyuls, or a California late-harvest Sauvignon Blanc.*

SAINTE-MAURE DE TOURAINE

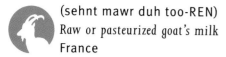

(sehnt mawr duh too-REN)
Raw or pasteurized goat's milk
France

One of the prettiest additions to a cheese board, a whole Sainte-Maure is a log-shaped cheese weighing about a half pound, its dimpled rind well covered with gray and white molds. Cut into it and you will find a surprise: a thin straw or dowel running the length of the cheese and sometimes visible poking through the ends. The dowel is a signature of Sainte-Maure, said to help hold the fresh cheese together and aerate the curd so it develops more quickly.

Sainte-Maure, as its full name indicates, comes from the Touraine region of central France, in the Loire Valley. Some Sainte-Maure is still made on the farm, but most of it comes from cooperatives or large dairies. The milk is coagulated slowly, using very little rennet and relying instead on the buildup of lactic acid to curdle the milk. The process yields a curd with a tangy flavor and a delicate texture.

The logs are usually coated with ash, but not always. The ash neutralizes the surface acidity, making the exterior more hospitable to desirable molds. Sainte-Maure can be sold after ten days, but it is usually matured for a few weeks to allow for more flavor development. The rind will become more thickly coated with mold and the interior will darken from white to ivory. At six weeks or so, the paste will be semifirm, dense, and smooth and a little creamy just under the rind, with a walnut aroma and an unmistakable goat's milk flavor.

WINES THAT WORK: *The region's wines match this cheese beautifully. Open a dry Vouvray or Sancerre if you prefer white, a Chinon or Bourgeuil if you prefer red. Sparkling wine is another fine choice.*

ST. GEORGE

Matos Cheese Factory
Raw cow's milk
California

Since the 1970s, Joe and Mary Matos have been making cheese in Sonoma County from the milk of their own small Holstein herd. Born in the Azores, an archipelago of Portuguese islands, the couple patterned their product after São Jorge, the aged cow's milk cheese of their homeland. Joe, a sixth-generation cheesemaker, tended the herd while Mary made the cheese by hand. Until the mid-1990s, when interest in American artisanal cheeses blossomed, St. George (pictured on page 58) was sold primarily in markets that catered to Portuguese immigrants.

Even with the attention and acclaim they have received for their cheese, the couple has resolutely refused to expand production, engage in promotion, or raise their price to what the market will bear. Consumers willing to make the trek can still buy the cheese direct from the farm at a relatively modest price. Mary no longer makes the cheese herself, but her daughter oversees production.

St. George is a firm, pressed cheese aged for three to seven months. Wheels range in size from ten to twenty pounds. The milk is not pasteurized but is subjected to heat treatment, a less severe process that removes some potentially harmful bacteria. The Food and Drug Administration considers it a raw-milk cheese, but raw-milk purists would not.

The wheel has a hard natural rind and a pale yellow to golden interior with many small eyes. A fresh-cut wedge has a dense, waxy, somewhat Cheddar-like texture; the aroma of fresh grass; and full, lingering flavors with firm acidity. Its sturdy nature makes it a great choice for a picnic.

WINES THAT WORK: *This cheese loves wine, and you can go in many directions. Among whites, good options include Sancerre, Grüner Veltliner, Chardonnay without obvious oak, and a dry German Riesling. Most reds will be harmonious, especially fuller-bodied wines such as Cabernet Sauvignon and Bordeaux. A dry amontillado sherry is close to perfect.*

STILTON

Pasteurized cow's milk
England

Produced since the early eighteenth century, Stilton remains England's best-known blue cheese and one of the world's finest. Only six dairies make it, and their cheesemaking practices are tightly defined to guarantee quality and uniformity. The cheese can only be made in three English counties, Derbyshire, Leicestershire, and Nottinghamshire, and it must have the traditional cylindrical shape and a natural rind.

The fresh Stilton curds are packed into tall cylindrical hoops with drainage holes, where they remain for five or six days, with frequent turning. After the wheels are unmolded, workers smooth their sides with a table knife to prevent air from entering. Then the young wheels move to an aging room for about six weeks. Flavors and aromas develop during this time, but the blue veins are still nowhere to be seen. Finally, the wheels are mechanically pierced and the blue streaks begin to emerge as the dormant *Penicillium roqueforti* spores added to the milk swing into action. Over the next few weeks, a golden crust will develop on these tall, sixteen-pound drums and the rivers of blue will snake evenly through the ivory paste, almost to the edges.

Most dairies release their Stilton at nine or ten weeks, but the wheels become creamier and more mellow with a few more weeks of age. At three to four months, Stilton will have a snowy dusting of white mold on the rind and a moist, creamy interior. The fragrance will be nutty and meaty, even a little smoky or baconlike, and the flavor will be rich and buttery. Look for Stilton from the Colston Bassett dairy, a premier producer.

WINES THAT WORK: *You cannot go wrong with port and Stilton, but a luscious off-dry amontillado sherry is a more unusual and equally enjoyable choice.*

Celebrating Diversity

Presented together, the cheeses on this platter represent a wide range of styles,
offering an enticing array of texture, aroma, and taste (see page 25).
Serve all seven listed here if your party is large enough, or choose as many as
five for a smaller group. For a dinner party where table space is tight,
you can cut and plate the cheese for each guest.

Boerenkaas

Brin d'Amour

Fourme d'Ambert

Hudson Valley Camembert

Humboldt Fog

Pleasant Ridge Reserve

Taleggio

< TOP PEDESTAL, CLOCKWISE FROM TOP LEFT: *Pleasant Ridge Reserve, Fourme d'Ambert, Taleggio;*
FRONT PEDESTAL, LEFT TO RIGHT: *Brin d'Amour, Humboldt Fog*

TALEGGIO

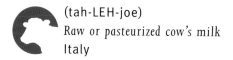

(tah-LEH-joe)
Raw or pasteurized cow's milk
Italy

One of Italy's few washed-rind cheeses, Taleggio has the thin, golden orange crust and the pungent smell typical of cheeses that have been repeatedly washed with brine as they age. The moist, salty surface attracts bacteria that take up residence and gradually break down the internal texture, working from the outside in. That's why a ripe Taleggio will always be creamier just under the rind.

Measuring about five inches square and two to three inches tall, Taleggio comes from a restricted zone in northern Italy and bears a stamp to prove it is genuine: four circles impressed on the cheese surface, three of them with a T in the middle. The rind is sticky and needs to breathe, so the cheese is shipped with a paper wrapper. It suffers in plastic, so if you purchase a plastic-wrapped piece, unwrap it as soon as possible and rewrap loosely in waxed paper, then store in a lidded container.

Traditionally, Taleggio was ripened in natural caves, but today most producers use temperature- and humidity-controlled rooms. The cheeses are ready in about forty days. To be legal for sale in the United States, raw-milk Taleggio must be aged for at least sixty days, so producers have apparently figured out a way to slow the development. Even so, raw-milk Taleggio is only rarely available here.

A ripe Taleggio will have considerable bacterial bloom on the rind and perhaps some gray mold. It will bulge on the sides and yield to pressure, signaling that the interior has softened. The ivory paste will be semisoft and silky, with pronounced aromas of meat, mushroom, and earth. The beefy, buttery, saline flavors are milder than you might expect from the smell.

WINES THAT WORK: *Spicy white wines and full-bodied reds are Taleggio's best mates. Pour a sparkling wine, Grüner Veltliner, or dry Pinot Gris, or consider the red wines of Piedmont (Barolo, Barbaresco, Barbera, Dolcetto) or an Aglianico from southern Italy.*

TOMME DE SAVOIE

(tohm duh sah-VWAH)
Raw or pasteurized cow's milk
France

Made by many producers throughout the *départements* of Savoie and Haute-Savoie, in eastern France, Tomme de Savoie is not a standardized, unvarying cheese. The wheels tend to weigh three to four pounds and measure about eight inches across, but they may be smaller or larger. They are typically aged at least a month, but often considerably longer.

Traditionally, many *tommes* were made from skim milk after the valuable cream had been removed for butter. The family kept this lower-fat cheese for its own consumption, saving the full-fat *tommes* for sale. Some producers still use skim milk for their *tommes*, but others use whole milk.

Like all the cheeses made in this region—Comté (page 52), Beaufort (page 33), and Reblochon (page 115), among them—Tomme de Savoie benefits from the abundant mountain pastures that cows enjoy from May through October and from the depth of experience of the local cheesemakers. It is a sturdy and reliable cheese, an everyday pleasure to enjoy with a salad or tucked into an omelet.

Tomme de Savoie is lightly pressed, which gives the interior a semifirm to firm texture, depending on age. With maturity, the paste darkens from ivory to butter colored to golden, and you can expect to find a few small eyes. The crusty rind should be dappled with gray, white, and gold molds, and the freshly cut cheese should smell pleasantly of roasted meat and moist earth, like a damp forest floor. The flavor will probably be milder than the aroma might suggest.

WINES THAT WORK: *The versatile dry white wines of Alsace come to the rescue again. Riesling, Pinot Gris, and Pinot Blanc all have the aromatic intensity and body to partner Tomme de Savoie, especially if the cheese is on the younger side. As the cheese matures and develops more earthy aromas, a medium-bodied red Burgundy becomes a better match.*

TUMALO TOMME

Juniper Grove Farm
Raw goat's milk
Oregon

A former corporate lawyer, Pierre Kolisch launched his small central Oregon goat farm in 1987, after a couple of years of apprentice cheesemaking in France. He has kept the operation small, milking about one hundred goats and making a variety of cheeses from their milk. For Tumalo Tomme (pictured on pages 20, 74), his signature cheese, the model was Tomme de Savoie (page 130), a firm, aged cow's milk cheese produced in the French Alps.

Kolisch follows the French procedures, albeit with raw goat's milk. The milk is curdled, cut, and stirred without cooking, then hand ladled into cheesecloth-lined molds. The curds drain for a day, coalescing into a wheel that can be unmolded and briefly steeped in a brine bath. The brine seasons the cheese as the salt slowly works its way into the interior, and it helps establish the rind. But the major rind development happens over the next two to five months in the aging room, as the wheels are repeatedly rubbed with brine and frequently turned to keep the fat and moisture evenly distributed.

Like its French namesake, Tumalo Tomme has a hard natural rind well populated with ambient molds. Inside, the paste is smooth, dense, and semifirm, with a number of small eyes. The cheese smells faintly of mushrooms and the forest floor, and the taste is mild and sweet, without the strong animal flavors or chalkiness that characterize some young goat cheeses. You might not even suspect that it is a goat cheese.

Kolisch makes only about forty-five four-pound Tumalo Tommes each week, so his cheese is always scarce and expensive. But it is worth seeking out to experience a handmade, raw-milk farmstead goat cheese, rare in this country.

WINES THAT WORK: *A medium-bodied red wine with smooth tannins, such as Merlot or Pinot Noir, will match Tumalo Tomme in intensity.*

VACHERIN FRIBOURGEOIS

(vah-sheh-RIN free-boor-ZHWAH)
Raw cow's milk
Switzerland

Resembling Gruyère in aroma and flavor, Vacherin Fribourgeois is smaller (fifteen to twenty pounds versus sixty pounds) and creamier. The curds aren't cooked, as they are for Gruyère, so they retain more moisture, yielding a smooth, moist, semifirm interior in the finished cheese. In Switzerland, Vacherin Fribourgeois is essential to classic fondue because it melts so well at low temperature. In fact, an estimated 70 percent of its production is destined for the fondue pot, a shame given Vacherin's likeability as a table cheese.

Made in the western Swiss canton of Fribourg, Vacherin Fribourgeois is a washed-rind cheese, about three inches in height and with a thin, golden or tan rind that you will want to cut away. The paste is butter colored and may have a few eyes. It smells of roasted peanuts and the flavor is robust, a fine balance of sweet and salty. Aging lasts for three to four months.

It took years for Vacherin Fribourgeois to receive its AOC status (see page 142), awarded only in late 2005. The authorities wanted to reserve the prestigious AOC for raw-milk cheeses, and one of the largest Vacherin Fribourgeois producers used pasteurized milk. But that producer agreed to switch to thermization (see page 143), a heat treatment less severe than pasteurization, and the officials agreed to amend the Vacherin Fribourgeois AOC to allow for cheeses made from thermized milk.

WINES THAT WORK: *Pour a fragrant, full-bodied white wine with a hint of sweetness, such as a California Gewürztraminer or Pinot Gris.*

VALDEÓN

(val-day-OWN)
Pasteurized cow's milk, sometimes with goat's milk added
Spain

With its blue-veined interior and wrapper of sycamore maple leaves, a wedge of Valdeón (pictured on pages 12, 110) commands attention on a cheese board. But only those with a fondness for big flavors will come back for seconds. One of Spain's most esteemed blues, Valdeón can startle tasters unaccustomed to pungency. Cabrales, its more famous neighbor, is considerably more aggressive, but both cheeses can test your mettle.

Made in a remote mountain valley in far northern Spain, Valdeón develops its blue veins during the six to eight weeks it spends aging in natural caves. In the first hours of cheesemaking, the fresh curds are sprinkled with *Penicillium* mold spores, which remain largely inactive until the young wheels are pierced to introduce air. The caves are not quite as humid as the ones in which Cabrales ages, which explains why Valdeón develops fewer blue veins in its ivory paste and less intensity.

Nevertheless, this cheese is no wallflower. Sharp and salty, with highly savory flavors, Valdeón lingers long on the palate. The texture is semifirm and creamy, yet crumbly, and the aroma is big and spicy. Serve Valdeón with roasted hazelnuts and a drizzle of honey if you want to tone down its piquancy. Some wheels are considerably more mellow than others.

WINES THAT WORK: *A tawny port or oloroso sherry has the rich sweetness needed to counterbalance a bold Valdeón.*

VALENÇAY

(Val-on-SAY)
Raw goat's milk
France

One of the classic goat cheeses from the Loire Valley, Valençay (pictured on page 92) stands out for its exquisite flavor and truncated-pyramid shape. Legend has it that the cheese was originally a conventional pyramid, with a pointed top, until it was served to Napoléon, who, angered to be reminded of his failed campaign in Egypt, pulled his sword and lopped off the peak. Like most cheese lore, the story stretches the bounds of credulity, but it may help you to remember what Valençay looks like.

After molding and draining, the fresh Valençay is turned out and lightly coated with ash, which encourages beneficial molds to colonize the surface. Within two to three weeks it is ready for sale, although it will continue to change positively for several more weeks. A well-ripened Valençay will have generous mold development on its surface and may even look a little wrinkled and saggy. It will be creamy under the rind, becoming progressively firmer toward the center but without a chalky core. The aroma will be faintly nutty, with no hint of ammonia, and a taste will deliver just the right amount of salt and tangy acidity.

The regulations for Valençay require raw milk. Because the cheese is rarely aged more than sixty days, the Food and Drug Administration minimum for raw-milk cheeses, it is no longer easy to find authentic Valençay in the United States. Some producers claim to have devised ways to slow down the aging and meet the sixty-day minimum, so raw-milk Valençay occasionally makes an appearance. But you are more likely to find pasteurized-milk renditions, which will bear brand names like Tradition du Berry (the historical Berry region is where the cheese is made), as they are not entitled to the Valençay name.

WINES THAT WORK: *White wines from the Loire Valley are the classic match, with good reason. They equal the cheese in intensity and weight. Look for a Sancerre or dry Vouvray, or from the New World, a Sauvignon Blanc or Chenin Blanc. Wines with herbal aromas are preferable to those with strong fruity notes.*

VERMONT SHEPHERD

Major Farm
Raw sheep's milk
Vermont

Cindy and David Major took over David's family farm in the 1980s, and began making cheese a few years later. Their objective was to create an aged sheep's milk cheese in the style of Ossau-Iraty (page 101), produced in the French Pyrenees. Their initial attempts flopped, but after a trip to the Pyrenees to visit traditional Ossau-Iraty cheese-makers, they refined their methods and almost immediately began winning awards.

Vermont Shepherd is a farmstead cheese, made only between April and October when the Majors' sheep are on pasture. They use a culture specific to Pyrenees-style cheeses, and once the curds have formed and been transferred to molds, a worker kneads the curds by hand to expel more whey and produce a tight, dense texture. After brining, the wheels spend four to eight months in the aging cellar, developing the flavor and aroma compounds that evolve only with time.

Wheels weigh about seven pounds and have a thin, hard, golden rind that may have some mold coverage. Internally, the cheese is semifirm to firm, with a golden paste that glistens on the surface and an aroma that fuses brown butter and coconut. You might expect more piquancy in a cheese of this age, but Vermont Shepherd is mellow and balanced, with a melt-in-your-mouth texture devoid of graininess.

In October, milking ceases and the ewes are bred. They will lamb in the early spring and spend a month nursing their newborns. Then, just as the Vermont snows melt and the fresh grass emerges, the young lambs are turned onto pasture and the ewes turn their milk over to the cheesemaker again.

WINES THAT WORK: *Many wines will complement this mellow, balanced cheese. Choose a dry white with some flavor intensity and body but without apparent oak or high alcohol, such as Pinot Gris, Chardonnay, or Viognier. Virtually any red wine with moderate tannin makes a good partner. An off-dry amontillado or oloroso sherry would be a less conventional selection, but a superb one.*

WENSLEYDALE

Pasteurized cow's milk
England

Made by a single creamery in Hawes, a village in Yorkshire, Wensleydale has had a tumultuous history. Cistercian monks began making cow's milk cheese in the vicinity as early as the twelfth century and eventually passed their methods on to the local farm women. Production remained a farmhouse endeavor until 1897, when a local merchant established a creamery at Hawes and began buying milk from the nearby farms to make Wensleydale on a commercial scale. His business foundered during the Depression and a succession of owners followed, ending—or so it seemed—with the closure of the creamery in 1992. But former managers stepped in to save the dairy and have succeeded in reviving a traditional, cloth-bound, matured Wensleydale that may well resemble what those late-nineteenth-century farm women were making.

Wensleydale Creamery now makes many cheeses, most of them aimed at the mass market, flavored with cranberry, onion, blueberry, and the like, and sold young. The serious cheese enthusiast will ignore these and look instead for the cloth-bound Wensleydale. The drum-shaped wheels range from ten to forty pounds and from three to nine months in age. The Special Reserve Wensleydale spends a minimum of nine months in the cellar.

At three to four months, a ten-pound Wensleydale has a well-developed rind; a moist, semifirm, ivory interior; and plentiful aromas of cheesecake and caramel. It is creamy and smooth on the tongue, like young Cheddar, with a tart, lactic finish. Serve with apples or a thin wedge of warm apple pie.

WINES THAT WORK: *A medium-dry Madeira makes an exceptional match for Wensleydale. The wine has just enough sweetness to soften the cheese's acidity and complementary nut and caramel aromas.*

Which Cheese with That Wine?

You've chosen the wine. Now, which cheeses to serve? The following guidelines will steer you toward the types of cheeses that typically complement each style of wine.

Sparkling wines, such as French Champagne, Italian Prosecco, Spanish *cava*, California *méthode champenoise* sparkling wine	**Mild to medium-intensity blue cheeses** Bayley Hazen Blue, Cashel Blue, Fourme d'Ambert, Gorgonzola dolce, Rogue River Blue • **Bloomy-rind cheeses** Brie, Camellia, Camembert • *Double-* and *triple-crème* **cheeses** Brillat-Savarin, Hudson Valley Camembert • **Washed-rind cheeses** Morbier, Red Hawk • **Hard aged cheeses** Boerenkaas, Lincolnshire Poacher, Mimolette, Parmigiano-Reggiano, Piave
Dry sherries, such as fino, manzanilla, some amontillados	**Hard aged cheeses** Dry Monterey Jack, Mahón, Manchego, Mimolette, Ossau-Iraty, Parmigiano-Reggiano, Roncal
Off-dry sherries, such as some amontillados, palo cortado, oloroso	**Nutty cow's milk alpine cheeses** Abondance, Appenzeller, Beaufort, Comté, L'Étivaz, Gruyère • **Aged cow's milk cheeses with caramel notes** Boerenkaas, Mimolette, Piave • **Other hard aged cheeses** Cheddar, Parmigiano-Reggiano, Vermont Shepherd • **Buttery blue cheeses** Cashel Blue, Stilton
Lean, fruity, high-acid white wines and dry rosés, such as Albariño, Chenin Blanc (Vouvray), Gavi, Muscadet, Pinot Grigio, Riesling Kabinett, Sauvignon Blanc (Sancerre, Pouilly Fumé), Verdejo, Vermentino	**Fresh or slightly aged cow's milk cheeses** Asiago (young), Crescenza, Mahón (young) • **Fresh or slightly aged goat's milk cheeses** Green Peppercorn Cone, Humboldt Fog, Sainte-Maure de Touraine, Valençay • **Fresh or slightly aged sheep's milk cheeses** Brin d'Amour, Feta, Monte Enebro, Pecorino Toscano (young)
Rich, aromatic, spicy, lush white wines, such as Chardonnay (white Burgundy), Gewürztraminer, continued >	**Nutty cow's milk alpine cheeses** Abondance, Appenzeller, Beaufort, Comté, L'Étivaz, Gruyère, Pleasant Ridge Reserve, Raclette, Tomme de Savoie • *Double-* and *triple-crème* **cheeses** Brillat-Savarin, Hudson Valley continued >

Grüner Veltliner, Marsanne, Pinot Gris (Tokay d'Alsace), Riesling Spätlese, Roussanne, Viognier	Camembert • **Washed-rind cheeses** Durrus, L'Édel de Cléron, Époisses, Fontina, Morbier, Munster-Géromé, Pont-l'Évêque, Taleggio • **Hard aged cheeses** Mimolette, Montasio, Piave, St. George, Vermont Shepherd • **Moderately aged goat's milk cheeses** Garrotxa
Light- to medium-bodied red wines, such as Beaujolais, Bourgeuil, Chinon, Dolcetto d'Alba, Grenache (Garnacha), Nero d'Avola, Pinot Noir (Burgundy)	**Fresh or aged goat's milk cheeses** Monte Enebro, Sainte-Maure de Touraine, Tumalo Tomme • **Nutty cow's milk alpine cheeses** Abondance, Appenzeller, Beaufort, Comté, L'Étivaz, Gruyère, Pleasant Ridge Reserve, Raclette, Tomme de Savoie • **Washed-rind cheeses** Fontina, Pont-l'Évêque, Taleggio • **Bloomy-rind cheeses** Brie, Camellia, Camembert
Full-bodied red wines, such as Barbaresco, Barbera, Barolo, Bordeaux, Cabernet Sauvignon, Chianti, Languedoc, Madiran, Merlot, Priorato, Rhône, Ribera del Duero, Rioja, Sangiovese (Brunello di Montalcino), Syrah (Shiraz), Zinfandel	**Aged cow's milk cheeses** Appleby's Cheshire, Asiago, Cantal, Cheddar, Dry Monterey Jack, Lincolnshire Poacher, Mahón, Montasio, Parmigiano-Reggiano, St. George • **Aged sheep's milk cheeses** Berkswell, Manchego, Ossau-Iraty, Pecorino Toscano, Roncal, Vermont Shepherd • **Washed-rind cheeses** Durrus, Taleggio
Dessert wines from botrytised grapes, such as Sauternes, late-harvest Sauvignon Blanc	**Blue cheeses** Bayley Hazen Blue, Bleu d'Auvergne, Cashel Blue, Fourme d'Ambert, Great Hill Blue, Rogue River Blue, Roquefort
Dessert wines with nut and caramel notes, such as amontillado, Madeira, oloroso, *vin santo*	**Blue cheeses** Gorgonzola naturale, Rogue River Blue, Stilton, Valdeón • **Hard aged cheeses with sweet or nutty notes** Berkswell, Boerenkaas, Cheddar, Lincolnshire Poacher, Ossau-Iraty, Piave
Port	**Blue cheeses** Bayley Hazen Blue, Gorgonzola naturale, Rogue River Blue, Stilton • **Aged cow's milk cheeses** Boerenkaas, Cheddar, Lincolnshire Poacher, Piave, Wensleydale

Cheeses by Country

ENGLAND

Appleby's Cheshire, p. 28
Berkswell, p. 34
Cheddar, p. 51
Lincolnshire Poacher, p. 83
Stilton, p. 125
Wensleydale, p. 137

FRANCE

Abondance, p. 26
Beaufort, p. 33
Bleu d'Auvergne, p. 36
Brie, p. 40
Brillat-Savarin, p. 41
Brin d'Amour, p. 43
Camembert, p. 46
Cantal, p. 49
Comté, p. 52
L'Édel de Cléron, p. 61
Époisses, p. 63
Fourme d'Ambert, p. 68
Mimolette, p. 88
Morbier, p. 94
Munster-Géromé, p. 98
Ossau-Iraty, p. 101
Pont-l'Évêque, p. 109
Raclette, p. 114
Reblochon, p. 115
Roquefort, p. 121
Sainte-Maure de Touraine, p. 122
Tomme de Savoie, p. 130
Valençay, p. 135

GREECE

Feta, p. 65

IRELAND

Cashel Blue, p. 50
Durrus, p. 60

ITALY

Asiago, p. 30
Fontina, p. 67
Gorgonzola, p. 71
Montasio, p. 90
Mozzarella di Bufala, p. 96
Parmigiano-Reggiano, p. 102
Pecorino Toscano, p. 104
Piave, p. 107
Taleggio, p. 128

THE NETHERLANDS

Boerenkaas, p. 37

SPAIN

Garrotxa, p. 70
Idiazábal, p. 81
Mahón, p. 84
Majorero, p. 86
Manchego, p. 87
Monte Enebro, p. 91
Queso de la Serena, p. 113
Roncal, p. 119
Valdeón, p. 134

SWITZERLAND

Appenzeller, p. 27
L'Étivaz, p. 64
Gruyère, p. 77
Raclette, p. 114
Vacherin Fribourgeois,
    p. 133

UNITED STATES

Bayley Hazen Blue, p. 31
Camellia, p. 45
Cheddar, p. 51
Crescenza, p. 55
Dry Monterey Jack, p. 56
Great Hill Blue, p. 72
Green Peppercorn Cone, p. 76
Hudson Valley Camembert,
    p. 78
Humboldt Fog, p. 80
Original Blue, p. 100
Pleasant Ridge Reserve, p. 108
Red Hawk, p. 116
Rogue River Blue, p. 118
St. George, p. 124
Tumalo Tomme, p. 132
Vermont Shepherd, p. 136

< *Fiscalini Cheddar*

Glossary of Cheese Terms

AOC: The abbreviation for *appellation d'origine contrôlée*, the French and Swiss system of laws that governs the production of certain cheeses to guarantee their quality.

Bloomy rind: Also known as mold-ripened cheeses, bloomy-rind cheeses, such as Brie and Camembert, have a coat of white mold. These molds help ripen the cheese from the outside in, softening the texture and enhancing the flavor.

Cloth bound: Some traditional cheeses, particularly Cheddars, are formed in molds lined with muslin or cheesecloth. When the young wheel is unmolded, it is encased in the wrapping and is referred to as cloth bound or bandaged. The cloth protects the rind and allows the cheese to breathe as it matures.

DOP: The abbreviation for *denominazione di origine protetta*, the Italian system of laws that governs the production of certain cheeses to guarantee their quality. The Spanish have a similar system and use the same acronym for *denominación di origen protegida*.

Natural rind: A hard yet permeable coat that both protects the cheese from excessive drying and allows it to "breathe" and mature. Natural rinds develop over time when the cheese is exposed to air; they do not develop if the wheel is waxed or wrapped in plastic. The rinds may consist largely of mold (Camembert) or bacteria (Red Hawk), or they may form underneath a coat of oil (Dry Monterey Jack) that protects against molds and bacteria.

Pasteurization: A heat treatment that destroys all pathogens in milk, pasteurization calls for holding the milk at a prescribed temperature for a prescribed time. Although pasteurization kills potentially harmful bacteria, it also destroys flavor-producing bacteria, which is why many cheesemakers prefer to work with unpasteurized, or raw, milk.

PDO: The abbreviation for Protected Designation of Origin, the European Union (EU) label for cheeses made in EU states that are subject to laws that guarantee their origin and quality. In essence, it is the EU version of AOC and DOP laws. For example, French Beaufort, which is an AOC cheese, would also be entitled to the PDO designation.

Raw milk: Milk that has not been pasteurized is known as raw milk. Many cheesemakers prefer it because it contains bacteria and enzymes responsible for flavor development. It also contains potentially harmful bacteria, but these bacteria typically do not survive the salty, dry, high-acid environment of an aged cheese. For that reason, U.S. law requires that raw-milk cheeses be aged for more than sixty days to be legal for sale in this country. These aged raw-milk cheeses have an excellent safety record. Some raw-milk cheeses from abroad meet the sixty-day aging requirement but are still illegal in the United States because the FDA considers them too high in moisture to be safe.

Rennet: A substance added to milk to cause coagulation, rennet is derived from the stomach lining of young dairy animals. Its active ingredient is the enzyme chymosin. Today, cheesemakers who prefer not to use animal rennet have other options for coagulants. Some of these coagulants are of microbial origin; others are genetically engineered.

Thermization: A heat treatment for milk that stops short of pasteurization. Under U.S. law, cheeses made with thermized milk are considered raw-milk cheeses.

Tomme: This French word, sometimes spelled *tome*, is applied to so many different types of cheeses that it is difficult to define. *Tommes* are usually small but not always, usually have a hard natural rind, and are made all over France (and Italy, where the comparable word is *toma*). Virtually every village in a dairying region has its own *tomme*, which carries the village or regional name, such as Tomme de Savoie.

Triple crème: In France, cheeses are designated as *triple crème* if they contain at least 75 percent fat in their dry matter (the cheese minus its water). Brillat-Savarin is a *triple-crème* cheese. A *double crème* contains between 60 and 75 percent fat in dry matter. Hudson Valley Camembert is a *double crème*, although these terms have no legal meaning in the United States. To achieve such high-fat levels in the cheese, the milk must be enriched with cream or crème fraîche.

Washed rind: Some cheeses are washed repeatedly during their maturation with water, brine, or a mixture of brine and selected bacteria. The washing creates a moist, salty surface that is inhospitable to mold but favorable to some flavor-enhancing bacteria. Époisses is a washed-rind cheese; its final washings include some of the local marc, or brandy.

Acknowledgments

I would like to recognize and thank the many people who contributed their expertise to this book: photographer Victoria Pearson and stylist Ann Johnstad for their mouthwatering images; Gretchen Scoble, Pamela Geismar and the design team for the elegant book design; Sharon Silva for her sensitive and astute copy editing; Laurel Leigh for her can-do attitude and deft project management; and Sebastian Craig at the Cheese Store of Beverly Hills for his assistance in securing the finest cheeses for photography. And finally, my thanks to Leslie Jonath and Chronicle Books for bringing such an enjoyable project my way.